Mind Bom

C000234657

Mind Bombs

Garrick Alder

Duckworth Overlook
London · New York · Woodstock

This edition 2008
First published in 2007 by
Duckworth Overlook

LONDON
90-93 Cowcross Street, London EC1M 6BF
Tel: 020 7490 7300
Fax: 020 7490 0080
info@duckworth-publishers.co.uk
www.ducknet.co.uk

NEW YORK
141 Wooster Street, New York, NY 10012

WOODSTOCK
One Overlook Drive, Woodstock, NY 12498
www.overlookpress.com
[for individual orders and bulk sales in the United States,
please contact our Woodstock office]

A catalogue record for this book is available
from the British Library

ISBN 978-0-7156-3766-1

Printed and bound in Great Britain by
Creative Print & Design, Blaina, Wales

Contents

For "Skipper":
one of the good guys

Foreword is forearmed

If you're looking for weapons of mass destruction, you won't find them here.

Weapons of mass destruction are nasty things. They're the reserve of governments who use them to hold civilian populations in obedient fear. The information age's weapons are much less noisy. They are weapons of mass deception and distraction. These are the comfortable myths and the shared presumptions that surround us daily but that we never even think about challenging – because they have become part of us. We can't even see them any more.

What civilians will find in this book are bombs that can be used comfortably and safely – they can even be lobbed from the safety of your favourite chair. Some are merely squibs and bangers, while others are grenades; some are landmines that won't even be noticed until someone steps on them; others are harmless-looking booby traps. Some are flares, that will briefly illuminate private darkness; some are simply unstable compounds that won't go off until someone stirs them; some might not even go off when they're meant to, but lie unexploded for years; some will be duds, and some are none of these.

The weapons on offer to you are made of information: the naive and the pedantic and the bizarre and the grotesque and the sincere and the insincere, the profound and the puerile. None of them will harm you, or anyone else – none of them is even 'forbidden'. This isn't another one of those books of the 'I could tell you but then I'd have to kill you' variety. All of this information is quite openly available if only you know where to look. And if you're reading this book, the chances are you don't know where to look. We all get like that sometimes. This book might help. It doesn't require specialist knowledge, it doesn't use long words (well, not often) and it doesn't play coy about its sources.

It may be hard to believe that things that are quite openly available are interesting or even theoretically dangerous. Would the 'powers that be' leave such knowledge lying about? Assuming you don't think the powers that be have bigger things to worry about, there are two answers to that question. The first is that you only remember what you recognise. As you'll see very early on, the interesting stuff slides past you every day, and you automatically forget it because you can't file it tidily in a pre-existing category. The second answer is: 'petrol'. To paraphrase John Taylor Gatto (whom you will meet later), you can walk into a petrol station and walk out with a jerry can full of an unstable compound with the destructive power of two sticks of dynamite – no questions asked. This highly flammable liquid has the power to propel a tonne of metal at nearly three kilometres a minute, and also has the ability to soak into clothing and seep under locked doors. But there aren't any restrictions on its sale, because petrol is needed to keep our society from grinding to a halt.

Ask yourself: how many innocent civilians are injured or killed by the deliberate and malicious ignition of petrol every year – and how many are injured or killed by custom-made fragmentation weapons used by national armies?

Now ask yourself: in the so-called 'information age', how many times have we been conned by those in authority, and how many times have we got them back?

Garrick Alder
December 2006

8

1: You and yours

It was known. But it was not known. That is, if you asked a knowledgeable journalist, or a political analyst, or historian, they knew about it. If you yourself went and checked the record, you could find it out ... In the information age there is so much information that sorting and focus and giving the appropriate weight to anything has become incredibly difficult. Then some fact, or event, or factoid, mysteriously captures the world's attention and there's a media frenzy. Like Clinton and Lewinksy. Like O.J. Simpson. And everybody in the world knows everything about it. On the flip side, there are the Fog Facts, important things that nobody seems to be able to focus on, any more than they can focus on a single droplet in the mist.
— Introduction to Larry Beinhart's *Fog Facts*, 2005

Where did all the Neanderthals go?

ONE HUNDRED THOUSAND YEARS AGO: Modern humans (*Homo sapiens*) shared the world with their closest relatives, Neanderthal people. Neanderthals had many adaptations to a cold climate, such as large braincases, short but robust builds and large noses - traits selected by nature in cold climates, as observed in modern sub-arctic populations. Their brains were larger than those of modern humans; they used bone, stone and wooden tools, and they produced art. On average, Neanderthal males stood about 1.65 metres tall (just under 5 ft 5 ins) and were heavily built, and muscular owing to their physical activity and robust bone structure. Females were about 1.53 to 1.57 metres tall (about 5 ft-5 ft 2 ins).

DECEMBER 2006: The Yangtze River dolphin is pronounced extinct after 20 million years. Marine biologists failed to find a single live specimen of the shy, blind mammal during a massive trawl of the Chinese waterway. Noise pollution from motorised boats is blamed for interfering with the dolphin's natural sonar and upsetting its navigation and ability to hunt.

1996: The Caribbean monk seal is officially declared extinct. It had first been spotted by Christopher Columbus and was hunted in the Caribbean for its oil and meat. It had no natural fear of humans and was exceptionally curious about passing boats. The last reliable sighting of this animal had occurred in 1952.

1990-1995: Tens of thousands of Bosnians are targeted and killed. The end of the Cold War had seen the unstable Mediterranean country of Yugoslavia split into six ethnic territories. This attempted extinction was a plan cooked up by the party of Serbian dictator Slobodan Milosevic, to create a racially homogenous 'Greater Serbia'. Eight thousand 'Bosniaks' died in one massacre alone (Srebrenica).

1994: In just 100 days in Rwanda, an estimated 1,000,000 Tutsi people are killed by Hutu people in the fastest massacre in history. The minority Tutsis had previously ruled Rwanda, but when they fell from power their perceived racism left them as objects of suspicion and fear for the Hutu.

1939-1945: An estimated 5,100,000-6,500,000 Jews are killed by orchestrated shootings and gassings in European territory occupied by Nazi Germany, after they are declared racially inferior 'enemies of the state' by German leader Adolf Hitler. Other targets of the state's drive for racial purity include the mentally ill, Communists, gypsies and homosexuals, an estimated 5,000,000 of whom are also murdered.

1915-1917: A total of some 1,500,000 Armenians are murdered by the Turkish Ottoman Empire. They have previously been identified as 'the enemy within' during Turkey's disastrous engagement with the Russians, after which legislation is passed allowing the 'deportation' of this fifth column. Thousands are forcibly marched until they drop of starvation or exhaustion, while some are shot en masse and others are blocked into caves which are then filled with wood smoke.

1900: The number of Native North Americans reaches an all-time low of 237,000 people. The number before Columbus arrived in 1492 is unknown but estimates range as high as 12,000,000 people.

12 AUGUST 1883: The last quagga dies in captivity. This South African cousin of the zebra (with striped head and shoulders only) had disappeared from the wild some twenty years previously, hunted to extinction for its flesh.

1768: Steller's sea cow disappears from the North Pacific. This enormous mammal – weighing up to 10 tonnes – was prized for its edible oils and fats. The first specimen had been caught just thirty years earlier.

1627: The last wild aurochs is killed in Poland. The aurochs was the wild ancestor of all modern domesticated cattle, which had been deliberately bred from captive aurochs (the male aurochs being legendary in its aggressiveness). The aurochs had disappeared from the isolated ecosystem of Britain during the Bronze Age but was widespread across the Eurasian landmass and could be found in Africa, India and the Middle East. By the 1300s, the aurochs could only be found in eastern Europe.

1600s: Central Mexico's native population now numbers around 1 million down from an estimated population of some 25 million before the arrival of the Conquistadores. At around the same time, a metre-tall flightless bird disappears from its Indian Ocean habitat on Mauritius. It had been isolated by evolution and had no natural predators. The dodo was naturally an inquisitive bird and – although noted for the poor taste of its flesh – it was easy to trap when the first western immigrants arrived, bringing with them cats, rats and pigs. Several species of Indian Ocean giant tortoise also ended their days in the cooking pot.

1500: The larger forms of wildlife on New Zealand are disappearing after humans arrive from the Polynesian archipelago. Among the disappearances are ten species of the giant moa, a 2-metre (6-ft) tall bird equipped with a sharp beak, which was both flightless and herbivorous.

500 BC-AD 500: On the Indian Ocean island of Madagascar, off Africa's east coast, the animals – including the pygmy hippopotamus, the giant tortoise and seventeen separate species of lemur – are disappearing after the arrival of human settlers. Some 2,000 large Pacific Island animals – including the giant grazing ducks of Hawaii – have become extinct since humans began arriving on the Pacific Islands.

30,000-50,000 BC: Modern humans appear in Europe. Neanderthals disappear from Europe.

Why is Mboy Dcik so hard to read?

Subject: Fw: Can you read this ???
Olny srmat poelpe can.

I cdnuolt blveiee taht I cluod aulaclty uesdnatnrd waht I was rdanieg. The phaonmneal pweor of the hmuan mnid, aoccdrnig to a rscheearch at Cmabrigde Uinervtisy, it denos't mtater in waht oredr the ltetres in a wrod are, the olny iprnoatmt tihng is taht the frist and lsat ltteer be in the rghit pclae. The rset can

12

be a taotl mses and you can sitll raed it
wouthit a porbelm. Tihs is bcuseae the
huamn mnid deos not raed ervey lteter
by istlef, but the wrod as a wlohe.
Amzanig huh? yaeh and I awlyas tghuhot
slpeling was ipmorantt!

if you can raed tihs psas it on!!

You may have seen this email and been amazed. You may even
have forwarded it on. You probably didn't realise, when you hit
'send' with an amused shrug, that you were spreading an idea
that has done more harm to English language literacy than
anything else in history.

Try reading these words, which are also anagrams with first
and last letters in place:

cleetrobain (11 letters)
cositabofun (12 letters)
patinailermaran (15 letters)

Even though the first and last letters are already in the right
place, you'll find the words get more difficult as they get longer.
And no, we're not giving you the answers. Work them out.

The brain is very good at sorting out anagrams where part of
the anagram is already solved. Figuring out what the whole
sentences mean is down to unconscious awareness of the rules
of grammar and sheer on-the-spot deduction. In order to
accomplish this, you need to know what the letters of the
alphabet are. That's the way reading should be taught, isn't it?
For most educational theorists, phonics – in which pupils are
taught individual letters, then the sounds they make, then how
to put them together into words – is king, and has been
throughout history. But 'whole word theory' (introduced in the
early 1900s) held that this was needless: the brain recognised

entire words without the need to break them down into letters. Pupils were now to be taught by flash cards. They learned to recognise whole words – but the very obvious side effect of this was that they could not recognise new words.

In 1840, literacy in the United States had stood at between 93 and 100 per cent. Around the time of the First World War, 'whole word theory' began to hit the classrooms. Of the 18,000,000 men who were tested for the draft between 1942 and 1944, 17,280,000 of them were judged to have the minimum reading competence needed to be a soldier (this represents a 96 per cent literacy rate).

In 1951, the national draft cranked up again for the Korean War – but this time 600,000 men were rejected. The US literacy rate had now dropped to 81 per cent.

The next year, the US Army – baffled by this sudden slump – hired psychologists to find out how 600,000 high-school graduates had successfully faked illiteracy.

One American educational historian described the results in the following stark terms:

> After the psychologists told the officers that the graduates weren't faking, Defense Department administrators knew that something terrible had happened in grade school reading instruction. And they knew it had started in the thirties. Why they remained silent, no one knows. The switch back to reading instruction that worked for everyone should have been made then. But it wasn't.

The Vietnam war began gradually in the 1960s and really got going after the JFK assassination in 1963. By the war's end in 1974, the number of would-be soldiers rejected because of their inability to read had reached 27 per cent of the total pool. A substantial chunk of the suitable 73 per cent only just scraped through as adequate; they could not follow topical events in a newspaper, read books for relaxation or pleasure, or write fluently.

How lies the land today? The National Adult Literacy Survey represents 190 million US adults (over sixteens). In 1993 it found that:

- 42 million Americans over the age of sixteen can't read. Some of this group can write their names and fill in height, weight, and birth spaces on application forms.
- 50 million can recognise printed words on a fourth- and fifth-grade level. They cannot write simple messages or letters.
- Only 3.5 per cent of the 26,000-member sample demonstrated literacy adequate for college study (30 per cent of US high school students reached this in 1940).

In plain language: 96.5 per cent of the American population is of mediocre reading ability or is actually illiterate.

No wonder they watch so much telly.

Bottom line: it is easier to learn to recognise twenty-six letters than it is to learn to recognise 10,000 to 20,000 individual words – the usual range of a phonically taught English-speaker's vocabulary. Next time that 'amusing' email appears, be a samrt psoren and bin it.

Discourse on Method

The 'Scientific Method' is (according to one online encyclopaedia) 'a body of techniques for investigating and acquiring new knowledge, as well as for correcting and integrating previous

15

knowledge. It is based on observable, empirical, measurable evidence, and subject to laws of reasoning.'

This, then, is the rulebook that has got us from alchemy to outer space in less than 300 years.

What is this marvellous method that can tease secret truth after secret truth out of the pullulatingly complex universe? Why isn't it available to laymen?

You'll be waiting a long time to learn it. There are no classes that teach it. It isn't handed out in a little souvenir wallet when you graduate as a physicist.

There is no such thing as the Scientific Method.

What there *is*, is a loose set of routines and logical sequences that are probably familiar to you already. 'Watch and wait' is one. 'If at first you don't succeed, try, try again' is another. 'If the results don't appear to be what you might expect, try something else' is a third. 'If the same method doesn't work the same way every time, then you're doing it wrong' – and so on.

The sorry truth is that the fabled Scientific Method is just that – a fable. Most scientists can rattle off a fairly good list of observational techniques and claim that this is the Scientific Method. They're bluffing. Ask a *group* of them to describe this alleged Scientific Method and you'll soon find confusion and discord.

If you have learned to drive a car, or have perfected a cake recipe, or have beaten a complex video game, you used the scientific method.

You're a scientist and you never even knew it.

1: You and yours

La, la, la, not listening

Why is the brain (or perhaps the mind – we'll come to that later) so bad at assessing its own abilities? Why, oh why are the stupid so damn intractable?

The answer is both simple and unpalatable. Ignoring unpleasant information is intensely enjoyable. Not just in the 'negative' sense that you simply don't encounter anything nasty. It is actively and positively pleasant.

In 2004, researchers from the clinical psychology department at Emory University asked staunch Democrats and Republicans to evaluate information detrimental to their preferred candidate prior to the 2004 Presidential election. The tests involved pairs of statements by the candidates, alleged President George W. Bush and his opponent, Senator John Kerry, in which each man had clearly and incontrovertibly said one thing on one occasion and the exact opposite on another (you know the sort of thing – 'Read my lips: no new taxes' followed by 'My fellow Americans, we're putting taxes up'). The test subjects were asked to consider and rate the discrepancy in each pair of contradictory statements in terms of severity.

Then they were presented with a third statement – a sort of mental band-aid – that might soothe away the contradiction – for the 'read my lips' pair, the third statement might have been something like 'The economic situation later took such a serious turn that keeping the original promise would have caused the country serious harm', for example. The scenario was repeated several times for each test subject. Meanwhile, the subject's brain activity was monitored. It will not be a surprise to anyone who has ever engaged in political debate that both Republicans and Democrats consistently denied obvious contradictions in their own candidate but detected contradictions in the opposing candidate.

As a 'control', pairs of contradictory statements from neutral figures such as actor Tom Hanks were also used. Democrats and Republicans reacted to the contradictions of these characters in identically disinterested ways.

Emory University's director of clinical psychology said: 'We did not see any increased activation of the parts of the brain normally engaged during reasoning. What we saw instead was a network of emotion circuits lighting up, including circuits hypothesized to be involved in regulating emotion, and circuits known to be involved in resolving conflicts.'

The test subjects on both sides of the political aisle reached totally biased conclusions by ignoring information that could not rationally be discounted. Shortly after that, activity appeared in the circuits involved in reward, the same circuits that light up when any fulfilling activity is undertaken. Having successfully ignored the blindingly obvious, the subjects were rewarding themselves with a rush of dopamine for doing so.

Ignorance is addictive and left-right politics is not so much a dialogue as two imperfectly dovetailed monologues.

Did I say that out loud?

In our dreams, people yield themselves with perfect docility to our moulding hands. The present educational conventions fade from our minds, and unhampered by tradition we work our own good will upon a grateful and responsive folk. We shall not try to make these people or any of their children into philosophers or men of learning or men of science. We have not to raise up from among them authors, educators, poets or men of letters. We shall not search for embryo great artists, painters, musicians, nor lawyers, doctors, preachers, politicians, statesmen, of whom we have ample supply. The task we

set before ourselves is very simple: we will organize children and teach them to do in a perfect way the things
their fathers and mothers are doing in an imperfect way.
— **Rockefeller General Education Board,**
'Occasional Letter Number One', 1906

Go to the top of class

We want one class of persons to have a liberal education,
and we want another class of persons, a very much larger
class, of necessity, in every society, to forgo the privileges of
a liberal education and fit themselves to perform
specific difficult manual tasks.
— **Woodrow Wilson (as president of Princeton**
University), addressing the New York City
School Teachers Association, 1909

In 1964, scientists finally began to inspect the way expectations
might colour schooling results. A consignment of rats was
obtained and divided into two separate groups for experiments
in maze-learning (you know the sort of thing – how long does it
take to learn the route to the cheese?).

The two groups of rats were handed to two different groups of
experimenters. Half the experimenters were told 'their' rats
had been specially bred from good maze-learning stock; the
other experimenters were told their rats were from rubbish
ancestors. Even though there was no difference between the
two sets of rats, the 'well-bred' rats performed better. The
next stop, inevitably, was the human subject.

An (unnamed) US school was subjected to a test grandly entitled
'The Harvard Test of Inflected Acquisition'. There were eighteen
classes, composed of children with above-average ability,
average ability and below-average ability. Within each of the
classrooms, 20 per cent of children were singled out at random

and subjected privately to IQ tests. Their teachers were told that the children's scores on the Inflected Acquisition test indicated that they would blossom educationally within eight months (remember, not even the teachers knew this was untrue). At the end of the eight months, the children re-sat their IQ tests.

Every single one of the selected kids scored higher the next time around.

Did you feel sorry for the fat kid?

Here's a secret that everyone knows. The people who were most likely to be in your school sports teams were bullies.

Surprised? Officially, you should be. For decades, the purpose of school sports (apart from the obvious 'health and well-being' stuff) has been to instil discipline and moral values in kids. In fact, kids who are keen on games are more likely to be thugs. Researchers from the University of Otago, New Zealand, monitored 1,000 people from birth and examined sporting participation and antisocial tendencies between the ages of fifteen and eighteen. They found that sporty kids were twice as likely as academic peers to be in trouble with the law by the age of eighteen.

Writing in the *British Journal of Sports Medicine*, co-author Dr Dorothy Begg said:

> It is considered that sports build character and that by participating in organised sport young people are exposed to strong conforming, rather than deviant, influences. They will thus become good citizens. Our study does not support the view that involvement in sporting activities is a panacea for delinquent behaviour. If anything, it indicates it may exacerbate the problem.

It is not known how often Dr Begg was chosen for netball practice as a child.

A problem shared is a problem spread

> The trouble with the world is that the stupid are
> cocksure and the intelligent are full of doubt.
> — Bertrand Russell (attrib.)

> So, first of all, let me assert my firm belief that the only
> thing we have to fear is fear itself – nameless, unreasoning,
> unjustified terror which paralyzes needed efforts
> to convert retreat into advance.
> — US President Franklin D Roosevelt,
> inaugural address, 4 March 1933

> I tell people, let's don't fear the future, let's shape it [*sic*].
> — Alleged US President George W. Bush, Omaha,
> Nebraska, 7 June 2006

Ever stopped and wondered why the world appears to be run by totally useless people?

If you haven't, perhaps you ought to. Put down this book and buy a newspaper instead.

But if you have wondered why this should appear to be the case, chances are your subsequent thoughts went one of three ways:

- 🔥 guilt at having such arrogant thoughts in the first place
- 🔥 rage at the sheer damn injustice of it all
- 🔥 simple disbelief of your own suspicions

The third option is by far the most likely. After all, how could the incompetent, inadequate and downright useless possibly rise to the top, time after time? How could it actually be true that the people who should be running the country are all driving taxis and cutting hair? It must be a trick of the light, so to speak.

It's not. The world really is run by useless people. It's just that they have confidence.

Do you find this hard to believe? That may be precisely because you are not useless.

In 1989, Cornell University psychologists Justin Kruger and David Dunning embarked on a study of the incompetent. Under the heading 'Unskilled and Unaware of It: How Difficulties in Recognizing One's Own Incompetence Lead to Inflated Self-Assessments', they set out to test four hypotheses relating to incompetent people, only one of which offered any crumb of hope. Incompetent people (they stated):

- will dramatically overestimate their ability and performance relative to objective criteria
- will be less able than their more competent peers to recognize competence when they see it – be it their own or anyone else's
- will be less able than their more competent peers to gain insight into their true level of performance
- can (presumably with considerable sweat and tears) be trained to improve their own skills and eventually recognize their previous incompetence

Kruger and Dunning first got forty-five subjects to complete tests relating to skills such as logical reasoning, language and grammar, and sense of humour, awarding 'scores' in each area. They then compared these results to the self-perceptions of the subjects.

They found that subjects whose test skills put them well below average believed that they ranked in the top third of the sample. The subjects whose test skills put them well above average, slightly (but consistently) underestimated their ability.

The stupid didn't realise they were stupid, and the intelligent didn't realise the stupid were stupid either.

The subjects were then faced with their actual test score results and again asked to estimate their own rank. This time, the competent group accurately estimated their rank. But the incompetent group – far from being crushed by realisation – still vastly overestimated themselves.
Kruger and Dunning noted:

> Top-quartile participants did not underestimate themselves because they were wrong about their own performances, but rather because they were wrong about the performances of their peers. ... [T]hey mistakenly assumed that their peers would tend to provide the same (correct) answers as they themselves – an impression that could be immediately corrected by showing them the performances of their peers.

What is not immediately obvious is where Kruger and Dunning found their test subjects. Well, research budgets are typically not large and the two psychologists took what was lying around in front of them. All forty-five subjects were students from the two psychologists' own Cornell classes – composed of some of the brightest young people in America, the psychologists and businessmen of the future. Kruger and Dunning, perhaps understandably, did not comment on the implications of this aspect of their research.

So who watches the watchmen? After analysing their students, Kruger and Dunning concluded:

> Our thesis leaves us with one haunting worry that we cannot vanquish. That worry is that this article may contain faulty logic, methodological errors, or poor communication. Let us assure our readers that to the extent this article is imperfect, it is not a sin we have committed knowingly.

Kid versus whizz-kid

Next time you're cornered by some starry-eyed convert to the wonders of the stock market, tell them a five-year-old girl could do better.

London-born Tia Roberts participated in a year-long experiment for 2002's National Science Week, in which she was given a fictional £5,000 to invest as she pleased. Also participating were City analyst Mark Goodson and 'financial astrologer' Christine Skinner. Mr Goodson relied on experience and computer analysis, and Mrs Skinner used the movements of the planets, casting horoscopes for companies based on the date when they were formed. Tia just picked companies with appealing names.

The point of this exercise was to see how well chance methods performed compared to professional forecasts. Strangely, the results of the experiment have not been trumpeted from the rooftops.

After one year, Tia had defied a 16 per cent fall in the FTSE 100, with her portfolio of shares increasing in value by just under 6 per cent.

Mrs Skinner's portfolio fell by just over 6 per cent (still out-performing the FTSE 100), although one wonders why she couldn't have foreseen this by the simple exercise of casting her own horoscope.

Mr Goodson, on the other hand, saw his investments dwindle by 46.2 per cent.

Tia described the feeling of beating financial whizz-kids as 'wicked'. Mr Goodson 'stood by his approach'.

Sweet sixteen, never been ... nah ...

Teenage pregnancies on the rise. Plague of sexual offenders. Moral breakdown of society imminent! Er ... no.

It's just that, for a lot of kids, puberty is happening earlier. One in six girls and one in fourteen boys has hit puberty by the age of eight. In the mid-twentieth century, this was one in a hundred. But today's children still end puberty at the traditional age – around seventeen years old. This means they have nearly a decade of hormonal stress to deal with.

Also (and more obviously) it means that children of primary school age are going through the first stirrings of sexual awakening. This finding came from a study that tracked a statistically valid sample of 14,000 British kids from birth. Dr Alex Mellanby of Exeter University said: 'You then have the situation where a 12-year-old mixes with 16-year-olds and is expected to have the same sexual experiences and reactions as them.' Dr Marcia Hermann-Gidden made similar discoveries when surveying 17,000 American kids in 1997. She said: 'This is proof that children are programmed to be sexual at a time when society still considers them to be very young.'

One British family planning expert has suggested fitting girls as young as ten with contraceptive implants. Professor John Guillebaud of London's Margaret Pyke Centre faced calls for his arrest after making his remarks at a family planning conference in 1999. Anti-abortion charity Life said: 'He should be arrested for aiding and abetting under-age sex, which is an unlawful activity. It is a green light to go ahead and be promiscuous. It is using children as guinea-pigs and that is child abuse.'

Stranger than friction

The number of strangers is reaching record levels. All that crap about being in and out of one another's houses in the old days, borrowing cups of sugar, is probably true. More than 70 per cent of people aged over fifty-five chat with their neighbours and more than half are happy to claim their neighbours as friends. By contrast, according to research undertaken by the Royal Mail, a quarter of people aged thirty-five or younger rarely or never speak to their neighbours. A third of them said they would not know their neighbours if they passed them in the street and have no desire to get to know them. This was confirmed in independent research by Dr Carl Chinn of Birmingham University.

Chinn found that a third of UK residents had not even met their next-door neighbours, suggesting that 'Poor neighbourhoods once had strong kinship, but now prosperity buys privacy.' But what is the price of privacy?

An estimated 80 per cent of parents now stop their children playing outside because of fear of strangers. The same number believe that their children spend less time playing outside than they did themselves as children. And you know what? They're probably right.

767,000: the number of empty houses in Britain

Fancy a house? Go out and get one, then.

There are empty houses everywhere: at the last count there were 767,000 in Britain – 3.7 per cent of all properties – and 128,000 of them were in London alone.

Most of them are owned by local authorities who have simply abandoned them to decay. Why not move in, apply for the electricity and water to be turned on, and embark on a little restorative DIY? Once you're in, stay put and make no attempt to pay rent.

The object of the exercise is to get what's called 'adverse possession' – you occupy a house quietly for twelve years, and once that period has elapsed you apply to the Land Registry for 'possessory title'. The property becomes yours to keep or sell.

In July 1999, jobless Timothy Ellis became the proud owner of a four-bedroom house worth £200,000 in Strathleven Road, Brixton, south London, after occupying it peacefully for sixteen years without paying a penny in rent, rates, poll tax or council tax. Lambeth council only noticed after ten years, and told him he'd have to move out. But they failed to instigate proper legal proceedings to have him evicted until four years later, and as a result he took them to court – citing Section 15 of the Limitation Act 1980 – and the house became his.

Neighbour Amanda Delaney told reporters:

> I wish I'd thought of doing what he's done, then I wouldn't be stuck in a two-bedroom house with five kids. He's all right. He's always friendly and says hello. It's the council's own stupid fault.

Lest you think that it's only scuzzbags and scroungers that occupy unwanted houses, British squatters have included Bob Geldof, Sting, Mark Knopfler, Joe Strummer, Richard Branson and Labour peer (and former leader of Brighton and Hove council) Lord Bassam. Further, squatting is not frowned on by everybody if it's done productively.

An English Heritage spokesman has commented:

Buildings are most at risk when they are unoccupied. Squatting can be very damaging, but in some cases squatters ensure that historic buildings are not damaged or destroyed and might even lead to their rescue.

Yet in 2004, some 380,000 people were unofficially homeless, according to the UK's homelessness charity, Crisis. This included some 75,000 people in hostels and 'bed and breakfasts', 220,000 forced to live with family or friends and 5,000 people who were about to be evicted.

In some ways, it seems, the complacent saying of the ignorant rich is correct: the homeless really just aren't trying hard enough.

£1,400,000,000 p/a: CRISIS's estimate of the cost of homelessness to British taxpayers

This is mainly composed of housing benefit and accommodation charges, but includes lost tax revenues from people whose homelessness means they are unable to hold down a job (and are therefore also paid unemployment or sickness benefits).

£230,000,000: the estimated annual value of heroin entering Britain that was controlled by just one Afghani family

The Baybasin family cartel was based on Canons Drive estate in Edgware, north London, where Huseyin Baybasin bought a house in 1994 – and he paid in cash. Which isn't surprising, since he was receiving and passing on some 4,200 tonnes of heroin every year – 90 per cent of the estimated total smuggled into the country.

One neighbour said:

They keep a very low profile. If it weren't for the sound of the front door being kicked down by the police from time to time, they would be pretty good neighbours.

No one knows how the Baybasin clan and its associates were allowed to emigrate to Britain in the mid-1990s, but *The Guardian* claimed to have uncovered evidence that Huseyin was operating in safety as an informer for HM Customs and Excise. As one senior detective said: 'We have enough organised criminals of our own without importing any more.'

£26,527,108,436,994: the total transaction value (gross) of debits and credits registered by the UK Home Office's accounting system in 2004

This is 2,000 times higher than the Home Office's gross expenditure for 2004-2005 and roughly two and a half times the GDP of the entire planet.

Chuck your passport

Getting a bit fed up with paying taxes? Why not start your own country?

You will need:

1. unclaimed territory, or territory that no one will bother defending (there's more of this about than you might think)
2. a name for your new country
3. a flag, national anthem and currency (optional)

Find your space. Claim it. No, this isn't as silly as it sounds. How do you think every other country did it?

In June 2004, a dinghy carrying gay rights activists plonked a rainbow flag on the largest island in the Coral Sea Island Territory, just off Australia's south-east coast. Protesting at the Australian government's decision to ban same-sex marriage, they proudly created The Gay and Lesbian Kingdom of the Coral Sea Islands, ruled by Emperor Dale I (AKA, Dale Anderson, then twenty-nine). The Kingdom – a constitutional monarchy, although the subject of succession has not yet arisen – covers around 2,500,000 square kilometres (1,000,000 square miles), and has adopted the euro as its currency. The national anthem is 'I Am What I Am'. Australia has so far done nothing in response, and the Kingdom is blithely issuing stamps and currency and offering holiday destinations, with diplomatic passports in the pipeline.

Or you can do what Paddy Roy Bates did: in 1967, he landed on a disused sea fort in international waters 10 kilometres (6 miles) off the UK's Suffolk coastline, and created the Principality of Sealand. Mr Bates, AKA HRH Prince Roy of Sealand, is in sole occupation with members of his family, which isn't surprising as the Principality – which has its own postal system and currency – has an inhabitable surface area of 550 square metres (6,000 square feet). Despite various attempts by the British government to snaffle Sealand from under Prince Roy's nose over the years, HRH is still on the throne and in 2001 it was reported that Britain had finally given up on the matter. And starting your own country can be profitable, too. Never mind the freedom to avoid taxes, mint your own currency and issue diplomatic passports. In 2006, Prince Roy put Sealand up for sale. Asking price? £65,000,000.

But you'd probably be best not to go as far as James Thomas Mangan of Illinois did on 1 January 1949. Getting well ahead of the looming space race, he annexed the whole universe (not including Earth) and renamed it the Kingdom of Celestia. Celestia (currency, the erg) scored its greatest success with a certain degree of UN recognition in 1958, when its flag was briefly flown at UN headquarters. Since then, it has sadly been downhill. With Mangan's death in the 1970s, the Celestian succession has fallen to be decided by his daughter Ruth Mangan Stump, 'Princess of the Nation of Celestial Space', and three grandsons, Glen Stump, 'Duke of Selenia', Dean Stump, 'Duke of Mars' and Todd Stump, 'Duke of the Milky Way'.

God save the Queen (from detection)

Queen Elizabeth II is a fraud. This has been known for years and nothing will be done. She'll still appear on the coins and stamps.

The problem arose on 17 April 1759 when George, Prince of Wales – signing his family name as 'Guelph' – married a pretty young Quaker named Hannah Lightfoot, the daughter of a London shoemaker. Their marriage certificate (signed by the Reverend James Wilmott and witnessed by Lords Ashburton and Chatham) is viewable at the Public Records Office in Kew, London. (It wasn't always – it disappeared for over two centuries.)

Eighteen months after marrying Hannah, George became King George III. Two months after that, he married Princess Charlotte of Mecklenberg-Strelitz and fathered the dynasty we have come to know and love. The only trouble is that Hannah Lightfoot was still alive when George remarried, and so their marriage was still valid (the Royal Marriages Act was not introduced for another thirteen years). This means that George III's marriage to Charlotte was bigamous, and all fifteen of their children – and their offspring – were illegitimate. George IV had no right to occupy the throne, his brother William IV was a fake, granddaughter Victoria was a phoney and Edward VII should have stayed playing cards. George V,

Edward VIII, George VI and Elizabeth II are all impostors. So where are the real claimants to the throne?

George and Hannah had three children, two boys and a girl. George Jnr adopted the surname 'Rex' and disappeared to South Africa – the name of his younger brother has been lost to history. Catherine went to live in Wales and married a Carmarthen doctor called James Dalton. If you're researching your family tree, you might like to look into this one day. But don't give up the day job. After all, the Queen has the army on her side.

£1,200: the British government's estimated value of the life of a hypothetical elderly woman with health problems

Compared to ...

£3,000,000: the British government's estimated value of an 'average' life

These two figures were drawn up by the Department of Health in 1998, for its Air Quality Strategy, which was published the next year. The AQS attempted to justify the costs of reducing pollution by comparing them to the 'cost' of the lives saved.

An apple a day

When doctors go on strike, fewer people die.

In March 2000, Israeli doctors introduced 'sanctions' in a dispute over pay. Only primary medical care was affected. Hundreds of thousands of visits to outpatient clinics were cancelled along with tens of thousands of elective operations.

Secondary and tertiary medical care (emergency rooms, dialysis units, oncology departments, neonatal care, etc.) went on as normal during the action.

Authorities therefore turned to the undertaking profession to see what effect this had had on the nation's mortality. They probably wished they hadn't.

'The number of funerals we have performed has fallen drastically,' said Hananya Shahor, the veteran director of Jerusalem's Kehilat Yerushalayim burial society.

Meir Adler, manager of the Shamgar Funeral Parlour, which buries most other residents of Jerusalem, declared:

> There definitely is a connection between the doctors' sanctions and fewer deaths. We saw the same thing in 1983 [when the Israel Medical Association applied sanctions for four and a half months].

How can this possibly be? In the United States the same year (2000) it was found that a conservative count had recorded 12,000 deaths from 'unnecessary surgery', 7,000 deaths from 'medication errors in hospitals', 20,000 deaths from what were referred to as 'other errors in hospitals', 80,000 deaths ascribed to hospital-borne infections and 106,000 deaths from 'negative effects of drugs'.

The total – 225,000 deaths-by-medic per year – makes being killed by doctors the third leading cause of death in the United States, after deaths from heart disease and cancer but ahead of those due to car accidents and lung disease.

2,000: the estimated number of Britons killed by over-the-counter painkillers every year

According to a research team from Geneva's University Hospital, the deaths are caused by stomach problems arising from long-term use, and the total is more than the number killed by cervical cancer or asthma.

Writing in the medical journal *Pain*, team leader Dr Martin Tramer said:

> These are wonderful drugs but they are toxic and there are alternatives which do not carry the same risk of gastric complications. If you want to take these for a short time to relieve joint or back pain, there's little to worry about. The risks are for patients who take them for a couple of months or more, for conditions such as arthritis.

Possible Lemsip side-effects

'Rashes, indigestion, bleeding from the gut, blood problems (unusual bleeding or bruising, sore throat and fever), loss of appetite, dry mouth, difficulty passing urine, tension, restlessness, disturbance of sleep, hallucinations, tightness of the chest, asthma.'

Made-up drugs

Virtually no scientific paper published about medicine is sound, reliable or relevant – according to one drug luminary.

Professor Richard Smith was editor of the UK's most influential medical publication, the *British Medical Journal*, between

1979 and 2004. In 1998, he beguiled the luminaries of the Royal College of Physicians by declaring that only 5 per cent of the entire planet's scientific papers came up to scratch. 'In most journals,' he said, 'it's less than 1 per cent. Many trials are too small to be relevant and many of the studies that are published are the positive ones – there is a lot of negative evidence that never sees the light of day.' He also highlighted the problem of fraudulent research, 'planted' on medical publications by pharmaceutical companies.

In one random sampling of ten international medical journals, Professor Smith found twenty-seven dubious studies. He said that this was 'the tip of the iceberg'.

In 2004, he left the *BMJ* – to become the chief executive of the European branch of US behemoth UnitedHealth Group (with revenues of £28 billion).

Professor Smith is the author of the book *The Trouble with Medical Journals*, in which he spells out his claims that the planet's medical journals have become 'creatures of the drug industry', rife with fraudulent research and packed with articles ghost-written by companies.

Nothing works better than Aspirin (so take nothing)

The placebo effect is that weird 'mind-over-matter' business where someone is told that a medicine will make them better, even though it's not really medicine at all – and because of the sheer power of belief, they actually do get better when they take it. ('Placebo' comes from the Latin meaning 'I shall please'. A scientific hoax isn't a hoax, because it's in Latin, you see.)

No one really knows why the placebo effect happens: it just does. If you disillusion the patient by telling them that their placebo is actually useless, naturally, their improvement usually ceases. There's also something called the 'noncebo', which has the opposite effect, making deceived people ill despite being harmless.

What is less well known is that placebos work even if the person taking them knows from the start that they are not medicine at all. In one study, fifteen neurotic psychiatric patients were told: 'We feel that a so-called sugar pill may help you. A sugar pill is a pill with no medicine in it at all. I think this sugar pill will help you as it has helped so many others. Are you willing to try this pill?'

Only one patient refused – perhaps giving his doctor a seriously funny look while he did so. The other fourteen all said 'Yes, please' (although what their true feelings were, we'll never know). At the end of one week, they had all improved – even to the extent of relief of suicidal symptoms.

The ring of confidence (tricks)

You're taking nuclear waste as medicine and you didn't even know it. It was never prescribed for you, and you never gave your permission. What's worse, you can't even refuse it unless you spend a small fortune on bottled water: you are exposed to an uncontrolled amount of tap water every day while brushing your teeth, drinking tea and washing your face.

Fluoride was added to tap water across the US and UK without any form of public consultation. Yet fluoride is known to cause skeletal disorders and poisoning of the nervous system. Fluorides are compounds of fluorine, the most corrosive gas in existence – a jet of it can make asbestos glow.

After the Second World War, the American Atomic Energy Program found that it had produced thousands of tonnes of fluoride waste that it couldn't dispose of safely. Relying on a single medical report that appeared to show a reduction in dental caries in an area with high levels of natural fluorides in water, the atomic scientists argued that they should be able to dump their waste in reservoirs. And they got their wish. And then other people copied them. As a result, you are drinking nuclear waste.

Purrranoia

Have you ever noticed that people who really like cats are a bit … odd? That they never stop going on about their pets, or fondling and even kissing them? Have you ever wondered why it is that the stereotypical 'crazy' person lives in a house full of the damned animals?

If you have wondered about the above, chances are that you're not one of the estimated 22 per cent of the UK population infested with the brain-parasite *Toxoplasma gondii*.

A paper published in the *Proceedings of the Royal Society* points out that the microbe infests rodent brains and facilitates its spread by removing the rodent's natural fear of cats. Some 35 per cent of the wild rodent population is infested with *Toxoplasma*, with their decreased fear of Felix manifesting itself in a suicidal attraction to the smell of cat urine. When the unfortunate (and normally timid) rats or mice are eaten, the parasite sets up home in the cat. From there, toxoplasmosis can be passed on to cat owners through microscopic amounts of faeces adhering to the cat's fur.

Dr Joanne Webster – co-author of the paper with Drs Manuel Berdoy and David MacDonald – said:

> It makes human victims more active and decreases neophobia – fear of novelty – and, in this study, decreased fear of cats.'

Colleague Dr Berdoy said: 'These results may explain the reports of altered personality and IQ levels in some humans.'

Sssssssssssshhhh

Between 50 and 60 per cent of Japanese men are smokers of cigarettes. In total, one third of the Japanese population smokes. Between them, Japanese smokers buy 900 million cigarettes every day, making Japan the third largest tobacco market in the world after China and the US. Only Greece has a bigger percentage of its population addicted to tobacco.

Yet Japan has one of the world's lowest incidences of lung cancer. The reason for this is the traditional Japanese diet: low in dairy produce and red meat, high in fresh fish and vegetables.

Speaking of a survey conducted by Japanese medics in 2001, the director general of the UK's Cancer Research Campaign, said:

> The most important thing anyone can do to cut their risk from lung cancer is to give up smoking, but for those people who are unable to quit, eating lots of fresh fish could be a useful way to moderate their risk. This research once again emphasises the important interaction of diet and tobacco in deciding whether we will develop cancer.

Predictably enough, no western health agency has chosen to emphasise the importance of this interaction.

In 2000, a research team, from St George's Hospital Medical School in London carried out breathing tests on 2,000 men aged between forty-five and fifty-nine, which showed that lung function is better among smokers who eat apples than among non-apple-eaters. Officially, no one's quite sure why this is. Predictably enough, it didn't get very much publicity.

1: You and yours

Dr Kenneth Denson of the Thame Thrombosis and Haemostasis Research Foundation, Oxford, spent ten years studying the health of smokers and concluded that it was not smoking but poor diet that caused 'smoking-related illness'. He said ten cigarettes a day are 'probably not so bad for you' and added: 'The risks attributed to the act of smoking, and especially of passive smoking, have been greatly exaggerated.'

Predictably enough, Dr Denson got lots of publicity. The Imperial Cancer Research fund described Dr Denson's statements as 'ridiculous ... Any competent scientist is aware that smoking causes lung cancer.'

Smoking is now being censored from television. One British viewer forced a complete review of Tom and Jerry cartoons, shown on children's channel Boomerang, after complaining that they were 'not appropriate' for young viewers because of scenes in which the characters smoked. UK media regulator Ofcom investigated and the channel agreed to edit out scenes that 'glamorise or condone smoking'. In its ruling, Ofcom stated:

> Following receipt of the complaint, Turner, the licensee for Boomerang, conducted an extensive internal review of the *Tom & Jerry* library to reassess the volume and context of smoking in these cartoons. The licensee has subsequently proposed editing any scenes or references in the series where smoking appeared to be condoned, acceptable, glamorised or where it might encourage imitation. We recognise that these are historic cartoons, most of them having been produced in the '40s, '50s or '60s, at a time when smoking was more generally accepted. We note that, in Tom and Jerry, smoking usually appears in a stylised manner and is frequently not condoned. However, while we appreciate the historic integrity of the animation, the level of editorial justification required for the inclusion of smoking in such cartoons is necessarily high.

Thank goodness no one complained about characters being put through mangles, set on fire, blown up, having their necks slammed in windows or their heads shrunk by swallowing alum.

"Patients often recognised normality when staff did not"

How can I tell that you are sane?

I can't. And in 1972, psychologist Professor David Rosenhan proved it. He took eight perfectly healthy people and got them to trick their way into mental hospitals.

They simply turned up at the admissions desk and reported that they were hearing voices. These supposed voices usually mumbled or were unclear, but distinctly repeated the words 'empty', 'thud' and 'dull'. The 'patients' were a psychology graduate student, three psychologists, a paediatrician, a psychiatrist, a painter and a housewife. None of them had a history of mental illness and the fake voices were the only symptom they described. Needless to say, all of them were admitted to hospital double-quick.

After being admitted, the subjects immediately 'stopped' hearing voices. The point of this charade was to gain entry to psychiatric wards and see how long it took before they were discharged by hospital staff. Seven of the fake patients received an instant diagnosis of schizophrenia; the other got manic depression (they were given medication, but quietly binned it when unobserved). Not one of the patients was detected by medics during their little holiday.

On the other hand, the 'impostors' had been instructed to keep careful notes on their treatment, and their copious note-taking tipped off genuine psychiatric patients almost at once. The 'fakes' found themselves accused (very nearly correctly) of being journalists and doctors, 'checking up on the place'. Meanwhile, this activity was interpreted by staff as further evidence of delusion: for example, the studious note-taking of one individual was listed as pathological 'writing behaviour'. At the same time, hanging around bored and hungry outside the canteen got another described as showing 'oral acquisitive behaviour'.

The stays of the fake patients ranged in length from seven to fifty-two days (the average was nineteen days). All were discharged with a diagnosis of schizophrenia 'in remission' – and then faced an uphill struggle getting the erroneous diagnoses struck off their records.

In his commentary on this terrifying game of blind-man's-bluff, Rosenhan wrote:

We now know that we cannot distinguish insanity from sanity. It is depressing to consider how that information will be used. Not merely depressing, but frightening.

How many people, one wonders, are sane but not recognized as such in our psychiatric institutions? How many have been needlessly stripped of their privileges of citizenship, from the right to vote and drive to that of handling their own accounts? How many have feigned insanity in order to avoid the criminal consequences of their behavior, and, conversely, how many would rather stand trial than live interminably in a psychiatric hospital but are wrongly thought to be mentally ill?

Once his results were made public, Rosenhan heard from a famous research and teaching hospital (which has so far escaped being named). This hospital claimed that the diagnostic 'errors' detected by Rosenhan's team could not be made at their institution. Rosenhan therefore arranged a sequel: the hospital was told that within three months, at least one of

Rosenhan's fake patients would attempt to gain admission. The hospital staff would rate incoming patients in an effort to identify impostors.

During the experimental period 193 patients were admitted. Forty-one were identified as impostors; a further forty-two were considered suspect. But all of them were genuine. Rosenhan had sent no fake patients at all. He concluded that 'any diagnostic process that lends itself too readily to massive errors of this sort cannot be a very reliable one'.

Perhaps this was the secret of German 'psychiatrist' Gert Postel, a congenital liar who left school as a dropout in 1979 and ended up as a top shrink on the strength of medical jargon he picked up from two female medical acquaintances. 'If you grasp dialectics and the jargon of psychiatry, you can put any old nonsense into a convincing form,' he said during his subsequent trial in 1999. Postel was so convincing that he became chief neurologist and psychiatrist at a regional mental hospital near Colditz, appearing as an 'expert psychiatric witness' at thirty trials. He was eventually rumbled by a patient who was also a judge – and who recognised Postel from a previous escapade in which he had posed as a lawyer.

While released on bail, Postel – who had been tipped for a chair in neurology – was made responsible for all referrals to psychiatric clinics, and supervisor of Flensburg's social psychiatric services.

Postel's secret formula was very simple. If a patient was sleepy or reluctant to speak, Postel diagnosed him as having 'a lightly autistic psychosis'. More lively subjects were suffering from 'active psychosis of a schizophrenic nature'.

You will notice that your local psychiatric ward still appears to be thriving.

Give a dog

If you have an unpopular name, you're more likely to get a pejorative diagnosis.

In a British study, psychologist Luke Birmingham picked ten popular names from records from 1974 and asked psychiatrists to rate them for attractiveness. Wayne and Tracey came out as most repellent and Matthew and Fiona did best. When Dr Birmingham presented other psychiatrists with a list of mental health symptoms exhibited by a fictitious young person held in custody by police, the speculative diagnosis depended upon the name Dr Birmingham gave the subject. Based on identical lists of reported symptoms, 77 per cent said that 'Matthew' was schizophrenic, but only 57 per cent said the same was true of 'Wayne'; 37 per cent gave 'Wayne' a diagnosis of personality disorder, drug abuse or outright malingering.

Bzzzt

In days gone by, when the television was playing up, you'd give it a good hard whack on the side. Nine times out of ten, the problem would be mysteriously resolved at once. In these more safety-conscious times, this is a technique reserved for the treatment of mental illness, especially depression.

Electro-shock therapy was invented in the 1930s as a treatment for schizophrenia, and is still used today. In the UK, up to 20,000 patients a year are sedated, with a muscle relaxant to prevent fractures during the inevitable convulsions, and up to 450 volts is passed through their brain. The aim of this is to produce a seizure, which sometimes appears to relieve symptoms of the original illness. No one knows why it works. When it works.

The UK's Mental Health Foundation refers to the 'brain damage theory' in respect of how it is thought ECT affects the patient. It says: 'Shock damages the brain, causing memory loss and disorientation that creates an illusion that problems are gone, and euphoria, which is a frequently observed result of brain injury.'

Of 1,344 psychiatrists surveyed by the Royal College of Psychiatrists, 21 per cent referred to 'long-term side effects and risks of brain damage, memory loss [and] intellectual impairment'. General practitioners reported that 34 per cent of patients seen in the months after receiving ECT 'were poor or worse'. And in a survey of ECT patients carried out by the UK Advocacy Network, 73 per cent reported memory loss and 50 per cent said that the ECT they received was unhelpful or damaging.

Are you entirely shocked?

Why do doctors have such bad handwriting?

OAP – Over-Anxious Parent
FLK – Funny-Looking Kid
TUBE – Totally Unnecessary Breast Examination
GROLIES – Guardian Reader Of Limited Intelligence, In Ethnic Skirt
NF(T) – Normal For (name of town)
GOK – God Only Knows
TEETH – Tried Everything Else, Try Homeopathy
FND – Fucking Nearly Died
SIG – Stroppy Ignorant Git
FITH – Fucked In The Head
PAFO – Pissed And Fell Over
TTFO – Told To Fuck Off

> — Popular codes written in patients' medical records, according to Dr Phil Hammond (*Private Eye* magazine's 'MD'), writing in the *Health Service Journal*, 19 December 1997

A spoonful of sugar

In general people are more the product of their environment than of their genetic endowment. This environment is being rapidly distorted by industrialisation. Although man has so far shown an extraordinary capacity for adaptation, he has survived with very high levels of sub-lethal breakdown ... Two foreseeable and sinister consequences of a shift from patient-orientated to milieu-orientated medicine are the loss of the sense of boundaries between distinct categories of deviance and a new legitimacy for total treatment. Medical care, industrial safety, health education, and psychic reconditioning are all different names for the human engineering needed to fit populations into engineering systems. As the health-delivery system continually fails to meet the demands made upon it, conditions now classified as illness may soon develop into aspects of criminal deviance and asocial behaviour. The behavioural therapy used on convicts in the United States and the Soviet Union's incarceration of political adversaries in mental hospitals indicates the direction in which the integration of therapeutic professionals might lead: an increased blurring of the boundaries between therapies administered with medical, emotional or ideological rationale.

— Ivan Illich, *Limits to Medicine*, 1976

This won't hurt

American and Norwegian hospitals used radiation to sterilise thousands of mentally disabled people in a twenty-year series of tests lasting until 1994.

Former director of Norway's medical health services Fredrik Mellbye said:

I cannot remember that anyone at any time put their foot down to stop what was happening. Authorities in the health services, psychiatrists and other doctors all knew what was going on.

The radiation sterilisation method was first used by Nazi doctors working at the Auschwitz and Ravensbrück concentration camps, and was used in secret joint US–Norway experiments aimed at assessing radiation effects. But – at the Nuremberg Trials and before – the Nazis called it the 'Indiana Procedure' because state-ordered sterilisation was an American invention. It was passed into state law by Indiana and national law in 1927, in the Supreme Court case *Buck* v. *Bell*, which saw seventeen-year-old Carrie Buck forcibly sterilised to prevent her 'degenerate offspring' from being born.

Other countries with an elastic concept of medical ethics:

Peru: sterilised 300,000 women with 'tubal ligations' (i.e. tying off of fallopian tubes) between 1994 and 1999. The sterilisations were aimed at poor women who often did not understand what they were agreeing to, or were pressurised into it.
France: sterilised 15,000 women without their consent in state-run hospitals during a four-year period ending in 1997.
Sweden: lobotomised around 60,000 children between 1935 and 1976 to modify their 'problem' behaviour.

Bzzzzzzzzzzzzzzzzzzt!

Would you trust your neighbours not to torture you? Probably.

Would you still trust them if someone ordered them to torture you? You'd be wise not to.

The 1963 Milgram experiment was intended to measure human willingness to obey authority figures, even when obeying orders conflicts with the participant's conscience. The experiment tricked volunteers into thinking they were delivering electric shocks of increasing magnitude to a helpless 'victim' (actually a confederate of the experimenter, acting a victim's part) whom they could hear screaming over a microphone link to another room, while a lab-coated technician (the experimenter) oversaw their actions.

In a rather interesting sidelight on the psychological ethos of the era that gave us *A Clockwork Orange*, participants were told by the experimenter that they would be participating in an experiment to test the effects of punishment on learning. The volunteers then had to read questions, and if the 'victim' got them wrong a shock would be delivered. In reality, there were no shocks. After a number of shocks at increasing voltage levels, the actor started to bang on the wall that separated him from the volunteer, complaining about his 'heart condition'. After some more shocks, the actor would fall totally silent. If at any time the subject indicated his desire to halt the experiment, he was verbally 'prodded' by the experimenter, in this sequence:

- Please continue.
- The experiment requires that you continue.
- It is absolutely essential that you continue.
- You have no other choice – you MUST go on.

Sixty-five per cent of Milgram's volunteers pursued the shocks to the 'fatal' level, though many were quite uncomfortable in doing so. Of the 35 per cent of participants who refused to administer the final shocks, not one tried to halt the experiment and not one left the room to try to check that the 'victim' of their shocks was alive.

Milgram – who had expected only around 1 per cent of people to administer fatal voltages – summed it up this way:

I set up a simple experiment at Yale University to test how much pain an ordinary citizen would inflict on another person simply because he was ordered to by an experimental scientist. Stark authority was pitted against the subjects' strongest moral imperatives against hurting others, and, with the subjects' ears ringing with the screams of the victims, authority won more often than not. The extreme willingness of adults to go to almost any lengths on the command of an authority constitutes the chief finding of the study and the fact most urgently demanding explanation.

Milgram reflected on one possible explanation:

The problem of obedience is not wholly psychological. The form and shape of society and the way it is developing have much to do with it. There was a time, perhaps, when people were able to give a fully human response to any situation because they were fully absorbed in it as human beings. But as soon as there was a division of labor things changed. Beyond a certain point, the breaking up of society into people carrying out narrow and very special jobs takes away from the human quality of work and life. A person does not get to see the whole situation but only a small part of it, and is thus unable to act without some kind of overall direction. He yields to authority but in doing so is alienated from his own actions.

My office – now

Psychopaths do better at work.

Most people, overfed on a diet of Hollywood films, associate psychopathy with murder and violent crime. The majority of psychopaths are non-violent. Some even work in offices. Like their murderous counterparts, they are manipulative and controlling, lack emotional depth and do not care about harming other people. In all, they are probably ideally suited to succeed in corporate culture, where each person is purely a discardable component in a bigger mechanism. Often, office psychos are charming, smooth-talking and personable. This is purely for display – the charm gets turned on in a flash when powerful people are about, and turned off again just as quickly afterwards.

Because psychopaths apply semi-scientific reasoning to social interaction, they quickly learn to fake the emotional responses that the rest of us use to communicate. The psychopath thrives quietly in the organised chaos of any business structure. People come and go, worrying about their own tasks and deadlines. The psychopath watches all this with the calculating eye of an alligator submerged in a watering hole, rating potential victims, planning how to get influential people on his side and always remembering weaknesses.

Professor Robert Hare of the University of British Columbia urges businesses to screen employees for psychopathy:

> The manipulative, arrogant behaviour of psychopaths often makes them prime candidates for promotion within large corporations built on ruthless competition. These are callous cold-blooded individuals. They don't care that you have thoughts and feelings. They have no sense of guilt or remorse.

Professor Hare said one per cent of the world's population suffered from a psychopathic personality disorder and that scandals such as those at Enron and WorldCom were caused by psychopathic executives.

So if you have a hundred people in your company, one of them will almost certainly be a living and breathing psychopath. But you probably won't spot them. They learned how to hide their real selves from everyone else long before they got near your workplace. And every day, they pick up more information about how to hide even better.

Psychopathy is regarded as not only incurable but untreatable, since psychopaths who have been through therapy merely use the experience to gain valuable clues about how to disguise their behaviour.

Professor Hare points out:

> Chief executive officers have to make decisions very quickly and they can't worry too much about the impact on individuals. Why shouldn't we want to screen them? We screen police and teachers. Why not people who handle hundreds of billions of dollars?

Corporate psychologist Paul Babiak puts the same matter another way:

> The psychopath has the ability to look like an ideal leader, because he or she can demonstrate those traits the organization needs and wants.

He puts the proportion of psychopaths twice as high as Hare:

> You can guess that 1 to 2 per cent of the people that you work with could have psychopathic tendencies. The psychopath is someone who comes across as smooth, polished and charming. The psychopath is the kind of individual that can give you the good impression, has a charming facade, can look and sound like the ideal leader, but behind this mask has a dark side. And it's this dark side of the personality that lies, is deceitful, is manipulative, that bullies other people, that promotes fraud in the organization and steals the company's money and does not help shareholders at all.

Babiak and Hare's book *Snakes in Suits* includes tips on mental self-defence for people who suddenly realise they're sitting across the office from a monster.

2: Politics by other means

Suppose that, in future generations, the most gifted minds were to find their soul's health more important than all the powers of this world; suppose that the very elite of intellect that is now concerned with the machine comes to be overpowered by a growing sense of its Satanism ... then nothing can hinder the end of this grand drama that has been a play of intellects, with hands as mere auxiliaries.
— Oswald Spengler, *The Decline of the West*,
Vol. I, 1918

Progress

1983: The microprocessor, which now costs in itself perhaps £20, is the heart of a computer. It has not yet begun to be applied: over the next 10 to 15 years, millions will be installed in industry, distribution, commerce.

Machinery, which has almost denuded the land, will now denude cities.

Politically, this will split the population into two sharply divided groups: those who have intelligence or complicated manual skills that cannot be imitated by computers, and those – a much larger group – who have not.

In strict economic terms, the second group will not be worth employing ... Unless some drastic change occurs in economic and political thought, the developed nations are going to be faced with the fact that the majority of

their citizens are a dangerous, useless burden ... There might be strong temptation on Governments to solve the problem by nuclear war. Doubtless, to salve consciences, it would be dressed up as a war between superpowers ...
— **Peter Laurie, 'The Impact of Latent Nuclear War on Democracy', Chapter 9 of *Beneath the City Streets*, 1983**

1997: The economic reality is that there are several million British workers whose labour power is no longer needed. Their role as labour has been stolen away by new technology, by the availability of much cheaper labour in Asia and South America, by the drive for higher productivity.

They are in the deepest sense redundant.

Looking at them from a strictly economic point of view, these former workers are worthless. More than that, they are an expensive burden – at least they will be if they are to be properly housed and clothed and fed, if they are to be given decent schools and hospitals.

So, why bother?

From a human point of view, of course, there is no doubt that they have value, just as much as any human, and that they all have a moral right to live secure and happy lives. But this is an inherent human value – nothing that the market can put a price on.

From an economic point of view, they are worth nothing. For these redundant humans, the creation of poverty is the final solution.
— **Nick Davies, *Dark Heart* [a study of the growth of British poverty], 1997**

Mary Shaw of Bristol University looked at population changes in Britain between the 1960s and 1990s and found that where populations had shrunk, the death rate was higher; conversely, where the population had increased the death rate was lower. Dr Shaw's report, published in *The Lancet*, concluded that longevity was linked to affluence. As some people became more prosperous, they escaped from areas of high crime, poor housing and variable healthcare. Those left behind tended to die younger.

The suicide rate is higher in deprived areas than in prosperous ones. For some inexplicable reason, the poor seem to suffer from fatal depression.

The UK's suicide capital is Manchester, closely followed by Hastings, Carmarthenshire, Pendle and Tameside. By contrast, of the thirty-eight local authorities that scored best – including South Herefordshire, Mid-Bedfordshire, Purbeck, Wokingham and Bromley – a third were classified as 'growth areas', attracting new residents.

Herefordshire recorded only four suicides between 1991 and 1996, compared to 208 in Manchester during the same period.

Adman of mass destruction

The conscious and intelligent manipulation of the organized habits and opinions of the masses is an important element in democratic society.

Those who manipulate this unseen mechanism of society constitute an invisible government which is the true ruling power of our country ...

In almost every act of our daily lives, whether in the sphere of politics or business, in our social conduct or our ethical thinking, we are dominated by the relatively small number of persons ... who understand the mental processes and social patterns of the masses. It is they who pull the wires which control the public mind.

The words above are intended as high praise, indeed as encouragement. They were written by Edward L. Bernays, father of public relations and nephew of Sigmund Freud. (The 'L' in Bernays's name didn't stand for anything – like US President Harry 'S' Truman, he put the initial there for effect.)

Quite apart from inventing psychotherapy, Freud had expended a large amount of his energy on mass psychology. In *Group Psychology and Ego Analysis* (1920), he stated that when an individual joins a crowd he ceases to repress his instincts, and thus relapses into savagery.

By 1930, in *Civilisation and its Discontents*, Freud drew from his theory the inevitable conclusion that human beings are inherently aggressive and decided that civilisation was in constant peril from the 'primitive' instincts of the masses. He wrote:

Civilisation, therefore, obtains mastery over the individual's dangerous desire for aggression by weakening and disarming it and by setting up an agency within him to watch over it, like a garrison in a conquered city.

The western world, which had just gone through the horrors of the First World War and was visibly on its merry way to the Second, absorbed this idea like gospel.

(It doesn't seem to have occurred to anyone that the 'primitive masses' only tended to revolt against oppression and that the mechanised mass slaughter of the 1914-18 war had been started by the supposed masters of civilisation and had killed only the sheep-like 'primitive masses'. Nor does it seem to have occurred to anyone that Freud had palpably – and perhaps inevitably – imposed his own upper-middle-class aspirations on the human psyche he was trying to map. The ruling class became Freud's superego, acting as conscience and role model, and the middle class became the ego – the average self, doing the best that it can according to its rulers. Beneath both came the id – a chaotic mass that had to be kept under control by the upper two layers if it was not to break out in madness. Freud's later projection of this three-fold model onto society probably only shows that Freud had recovered from a major neurosis.)

Into this atmosphere walked his nephew Edward. Bernays single-handedly created the Public Relations industry and simultaneously sold it to businesses and governments as a means of taming the primitive masses by pleasing them with trinkets. (QE very much D, you might say.) He wrote:

> If we understand the mechanism and motives of the group mind, is it not possible to control and regiment the masses according to our will without their knowing about it? The recent practice of propaganda has proved that it is possible, at least up to a certain point and within certain limits.

You may have heard of his 1929 Torches of Freedom campaign for Lucky Strike cigarettes: at a time when women were frowned upon for smoking, Bernays linked the idea to female emancipation. Using one of the world's first photo opportunities, Bernays arranged for female socialites to parade through New York, smoking their 'torches of freedom'. The result was a breakthrough for his clients, but sales were still not high enough. Further research – that is, opinion polls – by Bernays found that the would-be addicts were worried that the green packaging of Lucky Strike would clash with their dresses – so Bernays launched a further campaign to establish green as a fashionable colour by badgering dressmakers and dye manufacturers.

Where Bernays finally sold his soul to the devil was in helping American company United Fruit overthrow the newly elected government of the world's original 'Banana Republic'. United

Fruit virtually ran the impoverished central American state of Guatemala as a slave colony, paying a pittance to keep fruit rolling into the USA. When the reformist Guatemalan government of Jacobo Arbenz Guzmán attempted to rein in the company's power in 1954, Bernays planted articles in the US media, influencing public opinion and policy by tapping into the great 'red scare' of the 1950s and claiming Guatemala was about to join the Soviet bloc. With a sufficient head of public opinion behind the scheme, Arbenz's government was overthrown by turncoat Guatemalan army officers invading from Honduras, backed up by the CIA.

As proof that the good really do die young, Bernays lived to be 103, finally expiring in the 1990s.

How DO they get away with it?

In 2000, Hull University analyst Keith Meadows told a conference of polling analysts that questionnaires used to formulate government policies were 'hopelessly poor'. The reason, he revealed, was that the public was largely too bored, wily or dim to answer truthfully or relevantly.

He said: 'There may be a chasm between what people think they are being asked in surveys by official bodies and what they are really being asked.'

In 1998, a Gallup poll about the state of British politics included a rare control question to sift out bluffers and no-hopers and found that a quarter of respondents (24 per cent) believed William Pitt was a member of the Conservative Party's shadow cabinet. There have only ever been two William Pitts in British politics: British Prime Minister William Pitt was born in 1708 and died in 1778; his descendant, British Prime Minister William Pitt ('Pitt the Younger'), lived between 1759 and 1806.

A further three quarters of Britons sampled by the Woodland

Trust in 2005 thought that the Battle of Trafalgar was fought by the British Navy under the command of John Major in 1980.

A poll taken by Israel's *Yedioth Ahronoth* newspaper in December 2001 found that 76 per cent of Israelis supported Ariel Sharon's assassination policy of hunting down and killing Palestinians accused of terrorism. According to the same poll, precisely the same percentage of respondents thought the policy would either have no effect on Palestinian attacks, or would actually increase them.

Nearly 50 per cent of Americans believed that Iraq had weapons of mass destruction when this was used as a reason for invasion by the USA and UK in 2003.

One adult American in five thinks the sun revolves around the earth, an idea that science had disproved by the 1600s.

Seeking to improve its public relations, the Egyptian government conducted a poll in 2006 and found that 61 per cent of respondents had never heard of opinion polls. The poll also showed that only 10 per cent of those surveyed had taken part in opinion polls before; 49 per cent of those surveyed said that they would really like to be polled.

When US President Bill Clinton claimed in 1998 not to have had sex with White House intern (in UK English: 'work experience girl') Monica Lewinsky, most of Europe laughed. Clinton's defence was that his actions (that is, receiving a blowjob) weren't actually sex because no vaginal penetration was involved. This seemed like special pleading at the time – the desperate convolutions of a liar caught out. However, for some people, Clinton may have been telling the truth.

In a 1991 poll, 59 per cent of American college students – a democratic majority among the brightest of an entire generation – had agreed that oral sex was not in fact sex.

A report to this effect by Dr June Reinisch, former director of the Kinsey Institute for Research in Sex, Gender and Reproduction, was published in the *Journal of the American Medical Association (JAMA)* in December 1998, at the height of Clinton's persecution. For publishing Dr Reinisch's surprising information, Dr George Lundberg – *JAMA* editor for seventeen years – was fired during a telephone call to his home on 15 January 1999.

'His lips moved'

It isn't a crime for politicians to lie. And the fact that you aren't surprised by that shows that it ought to be.

Peter Oborne, political editor of *The Spectator*, urges that a new offence of political lying be introduced to rebuild public trust in politics. In his book *The Rise of Political Lying*, Oborne lists six suggestions to re-engage the public with a political process that is becoming increasingly surreal.

The first is for an independent British fact-checking organisation – along the lines of the Bank of England or the National Audit Office – which would act as a neutral arbiter on political disputes, publishing verdicts to prevent the public from being misled by spin and smears.

The second is for a very similar organisation, perhaps run by academics, to keep an eye on political bias in the media. Oborne comments:

> The modern British media has the power to make the world a much nastier and meaner place, and can use that power with horrible effect.
>
> It is right that they should be made much more accountable.

A new National Statistical Service is next on Oborne's wish list.

Statistics about Britain are collated by the relevant government department, meaning that they can be - and have been - warped by the wishes of ministers.

- Oborne demands a legally binding 'partition' between elected representatives and the civil service, to ensure that the machinery of permanent government can't be 'customised' by successive governments.
- He also recommends that ministers be forced to make policy announcements though Parliamentary procedure (as used to be the case) rather than to TV cameras (as is now so often the case).

The reason for this is that ministers who tell lies to Parliament can be formally challenged and have to face censure, whereas there is no mechanism for punishing an MP who lies into a reporter's microphone outside Parliament. (Once upon a time, long ago in the 1960s, a cabinet minister named John Profumo was caught out while lying to the House. He resigned and spent the rest of his life in obscurity, working for charities.) Oborne comments: 'Political lying is a form of non-violent assault upon the electorate, because it deprives voters of the ability to make a balanced and well-informed choice at election time.'

His last recommendation is that political lying be made a crime. Full stop.

Oborne asks the reader to imagine a crooked company that issues fantastic promises prior to flotation on the stock market, and the resultant uproar when it is found the company had deceived investors. He concludes:

We face a choice. We can either do nothing and carry on deceiving and cheating each other and wait for the public anger, alienation and disgust that will follow. We can watch the gradual debasement of decent democratic politics and the rapid rise of the shysters and the frauds and -

perhaps before very long – something nastier by far. Or we can try and act once more as moral human beings.

And then you wake up.

Don't watch my hands (#1)

There I was, in [Alistair Campbell's] office, and I said to him: 'Do you mind if we film what you are doing?' ... And he talked about various bit of paper, but it became clear to me that he was trying to push one particular piece of paper, or rather wad of paper, out of sight, while on camera. This wasn't necessarily a very bright thing to do. So I said: 'What's that?' And he said, 'Oh, that's nothing. That's just the message script.' 'The *message script*? What's the *message script*?' At that point he was rendered virtually speechless. ... That was the nearest we came in the programme to revealing something about what's called spin.
— Journalist Michael Cockerell, on filming a documentary inside Tony Blair's Downing Street; interviewed in *The Journalist's Handbook*, no. 63, October 2000

It is well known that everyone has a totally blind spot in the vision of each eye. What is less well known is that you have a big blind spot in your idea of reality itself.

The blind spot in your eyes is caused by the gaps in your retinas through which the optic nerves connect. The brain fills in the gap with information from the immediate surroundings of each blind spot and you never notice the join.

The blind spot in your idea of reality is far simpler. Your brain is a machine that makes sense of things. When information contain gaps, your brain estimates what those gaps must contain. And it does it so fast that you don't even realise it has happened.

This is the reason that the western world's courtroom oath includes (with 'the truth' and 'nothing but the truth') the stern injunction 'the whole truth': It has been known since time immemorial that it is easy to mislead people by not giving them crucial details. It is also the hardest form of deception to uncover, for two reasons.

Firstly, it can be used to conceal itself: unlike a direct lie, it does not lay itself open to being proved or disproved. Secondly, the person on the receiving end will find it very difficult to prove they have been actively misled, if they notice it at all – they have really been allowed to mislead themselves. And if the person omitting part of the truth gets caught out, well, who hasn't had an attack of amnesia about some crucial detail?

In 2000, a memo from Tony Blair to his 'communications team' was leaked to the BBC. It did Blair no harm at all, because there were very few people in Britain who actually understood what he was saying. It began:

> There are a clutch of issues – seemingly disparate – that are in fact linked. We need a strategy that is almost discrete, focussed on them.

After a series of petty-sounding gripes about various issues including law and order and immigration (which included the memorable line: 'It is bizarre that any government I lead should be seen as anti-family'), Blair turned his green ink to the matter in hand.

> All of these things add up to a sense that the government – and this even applies to me – are somehow out of touch with gut British instincts.

> The Martin case – and the lack of any response from us that appeared to empathise with public concerns and then channel it into the correct course – has only heightened this problem.

We need a thoroughly worked-out strategy stretching over several months to regain the initiative in this area.

This looks like English, but it isn't. Not, at least, as you or I might speak it. Pay particular attention to the words 'response ... that appeared to empathise with public concerns and then channel it into the correct course'. It doesn't say 'actually empathised with', but it does say 'the correct course'.

Brought back into the realm of plain language, it reads: 'People are losing faith in us. We need to perform some new tricks, pronto. And the way we're going to do this is not by listening, but by getting people to talk about what we want them to talk about.'

Forget the birds and the bees. It's time we talked about spin.

The analogy in the word 'spin' is with a cricket ball or a baseball: the bowler (or pitcher) delivers the ball in a way that makes its flight deviate from that which the batsman will be expecting. By this method, the batsman (the media) is forced to bat (interpret) the ball (the information) in a certain disadvantageous way. This works specifically with the broadcast media, for which time is at a premium and journalists struggle to make sense of facts against tight recurring deadlines. Newspapers – even the ones that actually try – don't really stand a chance against this onslaught: by the time they're on the scene, the original story is probably twenty-four hours old and everyone already 'knows' what has happened.

Let us return to Blair's memo, which goes on to outline some methods by which his longed-for 'thoroughly worked-out strategy' might be drawn up.

One of Blair's worries was that forthcoming crime figures would show a small rise:

The Met Police are putting in place measures to deal with it; but, as ever, we are lacking a tough public message along with the strategy [*sic*] ... Something tough, with immediate bite, which sends a message through the system.

On the family, we need two or three eye-catching initiatives that are entirely conventional in terms of their attitude to the family. Despite the rubbish about gay couples, the adoption issue worked well. We need more. I should be personally associated with as much of this as possible.

Remember, you were never meant to see this memo, only the results it demanded.

In psychology, the media art of 'spin' is known as 'framing': the practice by which a thought can be pre-shaped before it ever even enters your head. In this way, the entire public can be lured off down a side-street of debate, either talking about something the government wants to talk about, or wasting energy on something largely irrelevant.

A good example of the latter might be the hoo-hah that was ignited by Britain's former Foreign Secretary Jack Straw, who in mid-2006 sparked a time-wasting debate that is still rumbling on. Straw apparently suddenly decided that the time was right for a 'national debate' about the right of Muslim women to wear various kinds of facial covering.

Straw had been a member of Blair's cabinet but was sacked because he didn't please George W. Bush's government (the US has formally denied actually asking for Straw to be sacked; the UK has said nothing). Whether Straw's 'veil' idea was his own or someone else's is unknown. But it did happen at precisely the time that public opinion was beginning to demand some kind of national debate over who carried the can for the Iraq debacle. Whereas the Iraq issue was clouded, and complex, the veil non-issue pressed all the right simplistic buttons: it had 'mad

mullahs', it had 'oppressed women', it had 'sinister masked figures', it had 'civil liberties' it had 'integration' ... something for
everyone. Suddenly, the media were full of yes/no phone-ins,
and pro and con pieces. The beauty of it was that even the act
of questioning the reason for the 'debate' was to take part in it.

Sometimes, the framing is done so quickly that you learn the
'spin' without even having to think about it. These are the
ones you really have to watch out for.

Babies of mass destruction

When Iraq invaded Kuwait in August 1990, the western public
gave a big yawn. This sort of thing was quite common in the
Middle East. Iran and Iraq had only recently finished their
ten-year war. Israel seemingly invaded somewhere every other
week. Why should anyone care if one nasty dictatorship tried
to grab another one? Moreover, the second nasty dictatorship
had historically been part of Iraq, until a random post-colonial
carve-up by the departing British after the Second World War.

A month ticked by and the exiled Kuwaiti government – miffed
that public opinion wasn't blowing their way – set up a front
organisation in the US.

'Citizens for a Free Kuwait' signed a $10-million contract with
public relations giants Hill and Knowlton; Hill and Knowlton
arranged for a fifteen-year-old Kuwaiti girl, known only as
'Nayirah', to speak before the Human Rights Caucus of the US
Congress, which met in October. Nayirah told a heartbreaking
story. She had, she sobbed during her televised testimony, seen
Iraqi soldiers burst into the hospital where she worked and
throw premature babies out of incubators, leaving them to die
on the floor so that the equipment could be sent to Iraq. The
congressmen – and the viewing public – were outraged.
President George H. W. Bush publicly referred to her story six

times in the next month, to illustrate the wanton depravity of Saddam Hussein's regime. When the vote on military action against Iraq's invasion finally rolled round, seven US senators specifically mentioned Nayirah's story in speeches. The final margin in favour of war was five votes.

By the time it was revealed that 'Nayirah' was in fact the daughter of the Kuwaiti ambassador to the US and that her story (rehearsed to perfection with Hill and Knowlton's help) was total balls from start to finish, the war was over and no one cared any more. The End.

Grow your own terrorists

A dozen secret armies scattered across Europe were responsible for the deaths of thousands of innocent people after the Second World War.

Heavily funded by the CIA, the Gladio network had been set up by NATO to act as pre-packaged resistance cells in the event of Communist invasions. This was to be very much on the model of the French resistance during the Second World War: there would be bombings, assassinations, escape lines and provocations.

The Gladio 'cells' were set up in a dozen or more European countries, and they settled down to wait for the Soviet tanks to rumble westward. And they waited. And waited.

As it was, the invasions of Germany, Denmark, Turkey, France, Spain, Luxembourg, Belgium and Britain never actually happened. And the Gladio units – left twiddling their heavily armed thumbs – went slightly mad.

In Belgium in the early 1980s, twenty-eight people were shot dead in supposedly 'random' killings designed to be blamed on internal terror groups.

In Spain, Gladio took on the side of general Franco and secretly murdered his opponents.

In Turkey, some 5,000 trades unionists and immigrants were bumped off.

All of this remained secret from the civilian populations of the countries being used for a war game dress rehearsal.

To be fair, nearly every European politician was unaware of it, too. Every European politician who wasn't a part of it, at any rate.

In October 1990 Italian Prime Minister, Giulio Andreotti, officially acknowledged the existence of Gladio. He called it 'a structure of information, response and safeguard' and didn't refer to its role in undermining Italian democracy over the previous thirty years. (Mind you, with a new government installed on average every five minutes since the end of the Second World War, perhaps Italy hadn't really noticed that bit.)

On 22 November 1990, the European Parliament passed a resolution condemning Gladio, requesting full investigations in each country and total dismantlement of the paramilitary groups. Neither event has yet taken place.

Woodsmen of mass destruction

America planned to create fake terrorist attacks on its own soil in order to justify invading another country.

Operation Northwoods was a 1962 plan to generate public support for invading Cuba and the removal of president Fidel Castro.

The plan suggested various false flag actions, including:

- 💣 staging fake attacks at Guantànamo Bay and blaming it on Cuban terrorists
- 💣 deliberately sinking an American ship (empty, of course, although fake funerals would be staged later for TV cameras)
- 💣 'harassment of civil air, attacks on surface shipping and destruction of US military drone aircraft by MIG type planes would be useful as complementary actions'
- 💣 destroying a remote-controlled drone aircraft and claiming it was a commercial aircraft full of 'college students off on a holiday'

Northwoods was proposed by senior US Department of Defense leaders and presented to Secretary of Defense Robert McNamara on 13 March that year.

That was as far as it got.

President John F. Kennedy is supposed to have personally rejected carrying out Operation Northwoods. No official record of this decision is known to exist, but Kennedy removed the plan's author, General Lyman Lemnitzer, as Chairman of the Joint Chiefs of Staff a few months later.

Back, and to the ... right

For those unfamiliar with the case, US President John Kennedy was assassinated in Dallas, Texas, in November 1963. He was shot in the head with a rifle while riding in an open-topped car. A twenty-three-year-old former Marine named Lee Oswald was pulled in for the shooting, but was himself assassinated before he could be brought to trial. Virtually no one believes the official verdict, reached by the Warren Commission, which says that Oswald shot Kennedy with a mail-order rifle from a sixth-floor warehouse window (his fingerprints were found on boxes stacked near an open window).

The JFK case is widely regarded as the father of modern conspiratorial thought, and just about everyone has been fingered as a suspect. Until recently, the most popular theory has been that the CIA did it, to prevent JFK pulling US forces out of Vietnam.

But in 1998, researchers identified a mystery fingerprint that had been found on a cardboard box near the warehouse window back in 1963. It belonged to a convicted shotgun murderer called Malcolm ('Mac') Wallace, who was a personal friend of JFK's vice-president (and therefore successor), Lyndon Baines Johnson, a manic depressive whose mental illness, combined with the stress of his position, caused reckless and dangerous behaviour. Moreover, Wallace had been named as JFK's assassin in three separate confessions and legal documents before the fingerprint was identified.

Oddly enough, this news has had absolutely no impact at all on the mass media.

Gentlemen prefer greys

This bit is so outlandish that you may prefer to skip it. After you have read it, it will probably poison your mind to the extent you won't believe another word in this entire book. Then again, part of our aim here is to encourage doubts about predigested information, so what's sauce for the goose has to be sauce for the gander.

And since the human brain is so very good at forgetting uncomfortable information (see 'La, la, la, not listening') – you probably won't remember what it was about five minutes later if you do read it. So carry on – but don't blame me. I just report this stuff.

Just remember this: the following discusses a document that was really released under America's Freedom of Information

Act, and the Central Intelligence Agency (CIA) has never disputed its authenticity. Indeed, it has actually confirmed it.

Classified 'Top Secret – not for publication', the partially censored CIA summary records the results of an agent's eavesdropping on a telephone conversation between US gossip columnist Dorothy Kilgallen and her friend Howard Rothberg. It dates from 3 August 1962 and concerns a conversation the two subjects had recently had with actress Marilyn Monroe. The document records the claims – all of which have been verified by later historical research – that Monroe:

- repeatedly telephoned Robert F. Kennedy, US Attorney General and brother of US President John F. Kennedy, and 'complained about the way she was being treated by the President and his brother' (she was apparently having sex with both of them)
- knew about 'bases in Cuba' and 'knew of the President's plans to kill [Cuban leader] Fidel Castro'
- 'threatened to hold a press conference and reveal all', with reference to 'her diary of events and what newspapers would do with such disclosures'

Far and away the most interesting claim made in the transcript, however, is the claim that Monroe:

- said she had been taken by JFK to 'a secret airbase for the purposes of inspecting things from outer space'

Just two days after this CIA document was created, Monroe died at home of an overdose of barbiturates. The official verdict was suicide.

Well, you can't say I didn't warn you.

One of Milgram's 35 per cent

You owe your life to Stanislav Petrov.

On 8 June 1983, US President Ronald Reagan first christened Soviet Russia 'The Evil Empire'. On 1 September 1983, the Soviet Union shot down a Korean passenger jet that it mistook for a spy plane, killing all 269 passengers – including many Americans. Throughout September that year, the west began preparing a major NATO exercise called Able Archer, which centred on the hypothetical use of nuclear weapons in Europe. The Kremlin eyed it nervously, believing it to be a 'Trojan Horse' for an invasion of Soviet eastern Europe.

At 40 minutes past midnight on 26 September 1983 (still 25 September in the west), Lieutenant Colonel Petrov was on duty at the USSR's early warning headquarters at the Serpukhov-15 bunker near Moscow. If a nuclear missile attack by the United States showed up on his screens, the Soviet Union's strategy was to launch an immediate all-out nuclear counterattack. This was the Cold War game of nuclear brinkmanship, which was not called Mutually Assured Destruction for no reason.

The alarms suddenly went off, and Petrov saw a 'blip' on a screen that meant an American missile was on its way. Petrov suspected a computer error had occurred, since the USA would hardly launch one solitary missile to attack the Soviet Union and give away the element of surprise. He dismissed the warning as a false alarm.

A few minutes later the system indicated a second missile was approaching the Soviet Union.

Then a third.

Then a fourth.

Then a fifth.

Petrov had no other information than what the system was telling him. He had only a few minutes before he had to tell the Kremlin. He decided that he would trust his hunch and declare it a false alarm.

A few minutes later, the Soviet Union was not incinerated. Petrov had prevented a global nuclear war. But he had disobeyed orders by ignoring the computer warnings.

He avoided punishment but spent the rest of his career quietly in a less sensitive position and was finally pensioned off early.

Don't watch my hands (#2)

The newspapers of Paris, submitted to the censorship of the press, in 1815 announced in the following terms, Bonaparte's departure from the Isle of Elba, his march across France, and his entry into the French capital:

9 March: 'The cannibal has escaped from his den.'

10 March: 'The Corsican ogre has just landed at Cape Juan.'

11 March: 'The Tiger has arrived at Gap.'

12 March: 'The monster has passed the night at Grenoble.'

13 March: 'The tyrant has crossed Lyons.'

14 March: 'The usurper is directing his course towards Dijon.'

18 March: 'Bonaparte is 60 leagues from the capital.'

19 March: 'Bonaparte advances rapidly but he will never enter Paris.'

20 March: 'To-morrow, Napoleon will be under our ramparts.'

21 March: 'The Emperor is at Fontainebleau.'

22 March: 'His Imperial and Royal Majesty last evening

made his entrance into his palace of the Tuileries,
amidst the joyous acclamations of an adoring and
faithful people.'
— 'Vacillating newspapers', in *Ten Thousand Wonderful
Things:* A Victorian Anthology, 1889

The only people who have an interest in ignoring the phenomenon
of global warming are those who see only the economic problems
that might be caused to manufacturers and big business by a
switch away from fossil fuels. In 2003, someone leaked a PR
memo advising alleged US President George W. Bush's party on
'Winning the Global Warming Debate'. It began '"Climate
Change" is less frightening than "Global Warming"' and
continued: 'As one focus group participant noted, climate
change "sounds like you're going from Pittsburgh to Fort
Lauderdale". While "global warming" has catastrophic
connotations ... "climate change" suggests a more control-
lable and less emotional challenge.'

A very well-known, and much older, example of this gentle
metamorphosis is 'smart bomb', which has almost entered the
language and conjures up unconscious images of friendly and
thoughtful map-reading missiles scrupulously seeking out their
targets and only killing combatants. (This image persists in the
face of all evidence to the contrary. For example, in the 1990s
Kosovan war, only 2 per cent of 'smart bombs' hit their targets.)

'War on Terror' doesn't even stand up to that sort of scrutiny.
No one could seriously have believed that 'terror' could be
attacked with conventional weaponry, or even be eradicated
from the world by any means whatsoever. Nor could anyone
have really believed that war had been declared upon terrorists in general (who continued to strike with apparent impuni-
ty in areas of the world not encumbered with exploitable min-
eral reserves). What it appears to mean is, rather, that the
First World's general population must be prepared to suffer
sporadic guerrilla attacks, while occasionally watching tele-

vised military attacks on the Second and Third Worlds, the reasons for which remain unclear.

Another example is 'identity theft', which first surfaced in America in the late 1990s, and is currently being used to flog ID cards to a largely indifferent UK public. Calm yourself: your identity cannot be stolen. The necessary 'Invasion of the Bodysnatchers' technology simply does not exist. What can be stolen, however, is your money and your reputation. The practice of stealing these things was once known simply as 'fraud'.

Journalist Steven Poole has responded to this rising tide of verbal pondweed with a powerful study called Unspeak. The overtone of George Orwell's *Nineteen Eighty-Four* is deliberate: Poole recognises, as Orwell did, that thoughts are shaped unconsciously by the language in which they are expressed.

A friend of rational thought, Poole takes on the powerful and the pressure group equally: each one is trying to 'frame' the debate in their own terms.

On 'pro-choice', the bygone buzzword of abortion advocates, Poole remarks:

> The phrase carried unfortunate associations with the consumerist ideal of 'choice' ... Anti-abortionists quickly trumped that linguistic strategy by beginning to term themselves 'Pro-life', a term first recorded in 1976. The phrase 'pro-life' appeals to a sacred concept of life and casts opponents necessarily as anti-life, in fact pro-death. In a conceptual battle of two moral ideas, 'life' easily wins out over 'choice'.

Or again, on the name 'Friends of the Earth':

> This is a network of environmental groups in seventy countries. The name efficiently consigns anyone who

disagrees with their policies to the category of 'Enemy of the Earth'. An enemy of the earth must be a very nasty person indeed, a sci-fi villain like Ming the Merciless.

Once you have framed the language being used, you have imposed your own meaning on any subsequent debate. Even the word 'spin' is an example of Unspeak: what is meant by 'spin' is the art of producing a cross between deception and distraction – but there is no pre-existing word in the English language that defines this practice. This sort of presentational trick isn't especially new but what is new is the professionalism with which it is being carried out by people who were not formerly employed to pull the wool over our eyes.

Weather of mass destruction

The Vietnam war was caused by bad weather.

On 4 August 1964, the surveillance ship USS *Maddox* and the destroyer USS *Turner Joy* were patrolling the Gulf of Tonkin in rough seas, when a series of sonar 'contacts' suggested the *Maddox* was under attack by Vietnamese torpedo boats. This wouldn't have been altogether surprising, as the *Maddox* had previously deliberately provoked a genuine attack by coming too close to shore and then firing on the patrol boats that came out to inspect the ships.

A single sonar operator aboard the *Maddox* reported torpedo after torpedo, and the panicky crew radioed in their reports. There had been over seventy 'torpedo' traces claimed by this operator alone, but neither the *Maddox* nor the *Turner Joy* had been hit by a single weapon. Neither had either crew seen any boats on the mountainous sea. It was concluded that the excitement had caused the sonar operator to mistake the sound of his own ship's propellers for attackers.

The *Maddox*'s commander cabled the Pentagon immediately, describing the previously reported attack as 'doubtful' and urging 'complete evaluation before any further action'. But US President Lyndon Johnson went ahead and used the supposed attacks to secure congressional authorisation to launch a war against Vietnam.

In a televised address, he claimed:

> On August 2 the United States destroyer *Maddox* was attacked on the high seas in the Gulf of Tonkin by hostile agents of the Government of North Vietnam. On August 4 that attack was repeated in those same waters.
>
> The attacks were deliberate. The attacks were unprovoked. The attacks have been answered.

The Vietnam war had been on Johnson's mind for some time. CIA Operation Plan 34A authorising naval strikes against North Vietnam had been secretly approved by Johnson in February, six months earlier. The day before the supposed 'attack' on the *Maddox*, Johnson was asked in a press conference whether there was any substance to the claims of Wisconsin Representative Melvin Laird that Johnson was planning to attack North Vietnam. Johnson had replied: 'I know of no plans that have been made to that effect.'

Waterway of mass destruction

You will often hear the 'Suez crisis' mentioned as a key point in Britain's decline as an imperial power. Very few people, however, will tell you exactly what this 'crisis' was.

In July 1956, Egyptian leader General Gamal Nasser decided to nationalise the Suez Canal (that is, to take it over). The canal was, and is, the main artery for shipping between the

Mediterranean and the Gulf, which is the main reason that it was still owned by the Anglo-British Suez Canal Company despite Egypt's successful revolution against British occupation in 1952.

Facing international humiliation (not to mention loss of revenue), Britain started to plot ways of getting the canal back. In October that year, Albert Gazier, French Minister for Labour, and General Maurice Challe, a French Air Force Deputy Chief of Staff, met British Prime Minister Anthony Eden at Chequers, the prime minister's country retreat. There, Challe suggested nonchalantly that Israel should be encouraged to attack Egypt for some irrelevant reason and British and French forces could then seize the canal back under the pretence of restoring order. Eden gave a pusillanimous agreement, and the French went away and informed Israel of what they called the British plan.

Later that month, the French, British and Israelis met in secret in the Parisian suburb of Sèvres and agreed the plan of action. A week after that, Israel mounted an invasion of Egypt through Sinai and the Anglo-French clawback attempt kicked off, with troops mobilised across the Mediterranean. The British public was told nothing of the true object of the exercise at any stage. Nor (for nearly forty years) was anyone told that almost from the day Nasser grabbed the canal, Eden tried to have him assassinated in a series of cock-eyed episodes that surpass the infamously farcical CIA attempts to kill Fidel Castro.

Eden, over-medicated on prescribed amphetamines and under great stress, had been sent a memorandum by the Minister of State for Foreign Affairs, Anthony Nutting. The memo recommended greater involvement by the United Nations in the Suez affair, and suggested 'neutralising' Nasser's attacks on British interests through preventative measures.

Nutting was halfway through a dinner with the UN's Harold

Stassen when the telephone rang. Eden was almost beside himself:

> What's all this poppycock you've sent me about isolating Nasser or 'neutralising' him, as you call it? I want him destroyed, can't you understand? I want him murdered, and if you don't agree, then you'd better come to the Cabinet and explain why.

Eden later said much the same thing to the Permanent Under-Secretary at the Foreign Office, before apparently bypassing the Foreign Office altogether and going to the chairman of the Joint Operations Committee, Patrick Dean, a long-standing MI6 agent who shared Eden's view.

First MI6 attempted to get Nasser's personal physician to poison him, using *Daily Telegraph* correspondent James Mossman to deliver a £20,000 bribe. Mossman, who had worked for MI6 during the Second World War, delivered the bribe to the wrong man and the plan failed.

Next, MI6 obtained a dozen boxes of Egyptian 'Kropje' chocolates and experimented with inserting poison into them, ruining six boxes in trial-and-error attempts to disguise their tampering before succeeding. The deadly confections never reached their intended target.

After that failure, MI6 switched to a large-scale scheme: nerve-gassing Nasser's entire headquarters. They consulted with MI5's scientific expert, Peter Wright, who (in his memoir, *Spycatcher*) says he pointed out that 'this would require large quantities of the gas, and would result in massive loss of life'.

MI6 apparently abandoned this barbaric scheme at the planning stage, and turned to a modified poison-dart-firing cigarette packet designed by the Ministry of Defence's Explosives Research and Development Establishment. This device was tested on a sheep, which 'started rolling its eyes and frothing at the mouth' before slowly sinking to the ground.

After hatching such incredible plots, MI6 went traditional, and turned to hit men. A three-man team was sent into Egypt, but 'got cold feet', and left without completing their mission. A Cairo-based German mercenary was hired, but the Egyptians were tipped off, and the mercenary was 'believed to have been smuggled out of the country under [British] diplomatic cover'.

The attempted seizure of the Suez Canal all ended in tears for Britain a fortnight later, when America refused to become party to the deception and demanded a ceasefire.

Without the financial muscle to carry on in the face of withheld aid loans, Britain pulled out. Eden – who had experienced a nervous breakdown in the meantime – lyingly informed a hostile Parliament that there had been no collusion or foreknowledge, and then resigned.

Weapons of we are not amused destruction

The British government plotted the assassination of the queen and planned to blame it on terrorists. To make it even worse, the Queen in question was Queen Victoria.

In 1887 – the year of Victoria's Golden Jubilee – Britain was being shaken by the 'dynamite outrages' of Irish nationalist terror groups. Exiled Irish-American groups were launching attacks across London, killing six people in an attack in Clerkenwell and causing massive damage and panic at the Home Office, the House of Commons and eventually even Scotland Yard.

British police suddenly revealed the existence of what became known to history as the 'Jubilee Plot'. This was a plan to blow up Westminster Abbey during a service of Thanksgiving – with Victoria inside. The police claimed that this re-run of the Gunpowder Plot had been hatched by the New York-based Clan na Gael. The 'ringleader' of the plot, Clan na Gael member Francis Millen, was offered the sum of £10,000 to return to Britain to testify.

Letters found in a number of odd ways linked the alleged plotters to Irish MP Charles Parnell, who had been pressing the Commons for Home Rule and now found himself officially linked with a treasonous plot. The case against Parnell collapsed when the letters were exposed as forgeries, cooked up by a Dublin journalist and sold to *The Times*.

In 2000, it was finally revealed that Millen had been recruited by the British government to create a Fenian bombing campaign on mainland Britain. The scheme was intended by Prime Minister Salisbury to discredit the Home Rule movement and provide excuses for further crackdowns. Amid the genuine terrorist explosions that struck Britain as a result of this provocation, the Jubilee Plot had been run as a scare story, with the forged Parnell letters as 'evidence'. But unknown to his British handlers, Millen's efforts had cranked the Jubilee Plot into real life.

Two Irish-Americans carrying the necessary explosives only missed their appointment with Victoria because they missed a trans-Atlantic liner. They eventually arrived in Britain on the day of the service – but at Liverpool. At this point, a government commission was appointed to smother the evidence. The files containing the actual evidence disappeared from the Public Record Office until 1998, when historian Christy Campbell suddenly found them showing up on the system as though they'd never been away.

Labour peer Baron Hattersley has written:

> The 'Jubilee plot' is such a bizarre episode that I would regard it as the product of a febrile imagination had Christy Campbell not documented sufficient evidence to remove all reasonable doubt. His explanation of why Salisbury behaved in such an extraordinary fashion – the hope of both smashing the Fenian dynamite gangs and destroying Parnell by implicating him in the attempted murder – is convincing but not conclusive proof of the Prime Minister's involvement. But the detail – of both the bombers' movements and the machinations of the police – justifies a conviction.

The Fiat Uno had not yet been invented at the time.

£990,000,000: the amount by which taxpayers subsidised the British arms industry in 2001

£420 million of this goes on marketing, tax breaks and the export credit guarantee system (under which the government fully compensates manufacturers if purchasers default).

£570 million goes on subsidising the 90,000 jobs in the defence industry (£4,600 per job, per year).

£6,000,000,000: a Ministry of Defence overspend ...

... due to delays in the development of twenty weapons projects, identified by the National Audit Office between 2002 and 2004. These included the Type 45 destroyer (two years overdue), a crew-training aid for the Eurofighter (eleven months late) and the Eurofighter itself (more than a decade overdue).

What makes a Prime Minister tick?

'The successful candidate will have lost one or more parents in childhood, though he may be an admitted or suspected bastard ... He will be of a hypersensitive nature and will suffer from incapacitating psychosomatic illnesses, often at times of greatest stress.

'He will remain through his life isolated from his fellow men, nauseated by their junketings and exhausted by their relaxations. He will have been miserably unhappy at school and possibly so much so that he will never be able to bring himself to revisit it after leaving ... He will have been subjected to the intellectual, moral and spiritual domination of a disciplinarian mentor, whose commands he will in effect obey until the end of his days.

'Throughout his life he will maintain a regime of austerity, bordering on asceticism, outward forms notwithstanding, and often increasing in severity with time. Whether he is believer or not, he will have a deeply committed interest in religion. He will be subject to fits of prostrating depression. He will, if bereaved, be so desolated by grief as to render him totally incapable of maintaining his grip on life for a period ...

'He may be of a marked natural timidity and shyness, for which he will so overcompensate as to present on occasions an extremely aggressive front.

'He will possibly be peculiarly suspicious and credulous about magic and the supernatural and will take an extensive interest in fiery phenomena and storms.

'He will be haunted eternally by a compulsive and obsessive need for total love and adoration and support from another, and will continue to seek it until death, disregarding all else, even, on occasions, the security of state secrets, in his pursuit of it or its shadow, and probably writing a million words to wives, mistresses or sisters.'

— Speculative 'job advertisement' for the post of Prime Minister, drawn up by historian Lucille Iremonger in *The Fiery Chariot*, 1970, after surveying the lives of sixteen prime ministers from Spencer Perceval onwards

- intense control battles, very bossy and argumentative; defiance and anger
- resists affection on parental terms
- lack of eye contact, especially with parents – will look into your eyes when lying
- manipulative – superficially charming and engaging
- indiscriminately affectionate with strangers
- poor peer relationships
- steals
- lies about the obvious
- lack of conscience – shows no remorse
- destructive to property, self and/or others
- lack of impulse control
- hypervigilant/hyperactive
- learning lags/delays
- speech and language problems
- incessant chatter and/or questions
- inappropriately demanding and/or clingy
- food issues – hordes, gorges, refuses to eat, eats strange things, hides food
- fascinated with fire, blood, gore, weapons, evil
- very concerned about tiny hurts but brushes off big hurts

— Symptoms of Reactive Attachment Disorder, a severe personality disorder found in people who experienced childhood loss of a parent or primary caregiver

82

The which Blair project

We all know that politicians are not the same as us.

Tony Blair – who was so badly misadvised when he conferred with God over the invasion of Iraq – has come under the especial scrutiny of armchair psychologists, mainly as a result of his habitual distortion of the truth and confusion of belief and fact, examples of which do not need rehearsing here. In 2003, after the Iraq debacle was well and truly under way, *Times* columnist Matthew Parris said Blair's grasp on reality was weakening; the *New Statesman* quoted a psychotherapist who said Blair had a 'devious personality'; and a psychologist at Oxford University called Blair a 'plausible psychopath'.

In December that year, the *Journal of the Royal Society of Medicine* published an article by Dr Allan Beveridge, which concluded: 'Is the prime minister mad? Without more information, the psychiatrist's answer has to be "I don't know".' Despite his stern refusal to diagnose without encounter, Beveridge effectively ruled out psychopathy:

> The qualities that have been cited to prove that Blair is a psychopath are his charm, insincerity and talent for drama … The most prosaic explanation for these qualities is that he is a lawyer, merely using the tricks of the trade to argue the case. He has the lawyer's ability to defend positions without necessarily believing in them.

(This is not actually much of a defence of an elected representative – nor, of course, does it rule out the possibility that psychopaths can make very good lawyers). Interestingly, Dr Beveridge concluded:

> However, it could be argued there is something in the lay view that high office has driven Tony Blair, like some of his predecessors, to the edge of madness.

That political life can have an adverse effect upon mental health is so apparent that it hardly needs to be commented upon. In times of war, the pressure can become too much: one thinks of Anthony Eden nearly unhinged by Suez, or Churchill's swings between blackest depression and euphoria.

There is also the (still unresolved) issue of John Major's alleged nervous breakdown during the ERM debacle. If this was a true nervous breakdown in the sense of a psychiatric 'episode', it was very quickly resolved, and the more likely explanation for the rumours is that Major suffered a crisis of self-confidence and withdrew temporarily from communication with colleagues.

This is not, however, to confuse the pressures of the job with the state of the mind that takes on the job in the first place. Dr Beveridge's disavowal of psychopathy may well be right – the traditional variety of psychopath is usually too disorganised to 'get on' in politics in a normal democracy. That is not to say that there are no psychopaths in politics. The socially well-adjusted psychopath – with his freedom from guilt, neuroses, inhibitions – is a socially charming and ruthless operator who is ideally equipped to climb in politics, where friendship is only temporary and people are only tools.

Our current political system could well be acting as a self-service buffet for well-adjusted psychopaths. Jeremy Paxman in his survey of *The Political Animal* quotes psychiatrist Anthony Storr, 'who counted a number of politicians among his clients':

One or two of the politicians I met were virtual psychopaths. Anything – even if it was a wife or children – which got in the way of their advancement was just dispensed with.

Nevertheless, in ruling out psychopathy and yet refusing to embrace a claim of job-induced psychosis (or related disorder), Dr Beveridge was forcing a false choice on his readers. The question Dr Beveridge did not ask was whether the post of prime minister tended to attract a certain sort of candidate. The childhood of Tony Blair is suggestive.

His father Leo (troubled by his own parentage) uprooted the family time and again, moving the infant Blair from Edinburgh to Glasgow, to Australia, back to Durham. Blair himself has said: 'We moved around a lot ... I never felt myself very anchored in a particular setting or class.' He also concedes that Blair senior's stroke (when Blair was ten) was 'one of the formative events' in his life.

Psychoanalytical scholar and former Labour MP Leo Abse takes his lead from Freud, rooting Blair's trauma in his father's stroke, which ended his ambition of becoming a Conservative MP. The Oedipus complex, as is well known, consists of a boy's subconscious desire for removal of the father who currently possesses the mother.

'And what if,' Abse writes, 'death strikes but does not slay, leaving the victim dumb but with accusatory eyes staring for years, day in and day out, at his wretched little son, denied the relief of mourning ... [?]'

It was during this stage that Blair's trademark phoney smile first appeared, directed first at his teachers, and was (Abse writes) 'successfully used to deflect any potential hostility and which [smile] now he still so notoriously deploys and which indeed has become his political trademark'. Abse judges that this compulsive smile 'falls into the category that the insightful research psychotherapist Valerie Sinason has identified among patients suffering from severe emotional traumas and severe physical disabilities'.

Sinason herself describes it thusly:

> By exaggerating a speech defect, or lack of language knowledge, or handicapped walk, the learning disabled

person is able to feel they have some control over their handicap.

Also, they achieve a narcissistic victory over non-handicapped people by fooling them into believing the exaggerated speech or walk is their real voice or real walk. *Frequently, the defence mechanism takes the form of an appeasing, handicapped smile to create a false, happy self and keep the outer world happy with them.*

Abse locates in Blair a tendency towards conflict avoidance, as suggested by the phoney smile: indeed, it suggests that Blair's phoney smile (as opposed to the real one, which is occasionally seen) is a sign of when he is at his unhappiest. The Clause IV vote, the 'third way', the failed merger with the Lib Dems – all these, Abse suggests, are Blair reshaping the world around him to avoid clashes. On the other hand, when Blair's impulses are permitted expression (under the guidance of another and when he can be sure of winning hands down), international law will not be allowed to get in the way of a Kosovo or an Iraq. Nor can personal scruples get in the way of surreptitiously smearing a Dr David Kelly.

During Blair senior's prolonged recovery, Blair's mother (an all but invisible presence in Blair's biography) held the family together with devoutly religious behaviour. Blair has admitted that he came to 'take up the standard' that his father had dropped, and felt his father's political ambitions transfer on to him. After this came Still's disease, a form of rheumatoid arthritis, which attacked Blair's sister Sarah, causing her to spend two years in hospital. Blair, suggests Abse:

Therefore entered his teens fearful that he was being pursued, frightened that he would be the next victim of a hostile invisible disabler intent on mowing down the family. The Terminator struck yet again. Cancer attacked the thyroid of his mother; for five years she bravely struggled, in and out of hospital, before dying when Tony was twenty-two years old.

Blair withdrew into himself and took to obsessive Bible study, the roots of his much-vaunted Christianity. The rest we know.

The question in all this is not whether Blair's mind has suffered as a result of repeated childhood trauma, but the degree to which it has suffered. Only Blair's psychiatrist could know, but the widespread and published suspicion might seem to suggest that Blair's behaviour is a dead giveaway.

Matthew Parris later restated his case more strongly:

> I believe Tony Blair is ... close to being unhinged. I said from the start that there was something wrong in his head, and each passing year convinces me more strongly that this man is a pathological confidence-trickster. To the extent that he ever believes what he says, he is delusional.
>
> To the extent that he does not, he is an actor whose first invention – himself – has been his only interesting role.

The things they say (#1)

'It is clear the US authorities did little or nothing to pre-empt the events of 9/11. It is known that at least 11 countries provided advance warning to the US of the 9/11 attacks. Two senior Mossad experts alerted the CIA and FBI to a cell of 200 terrorists said to be preparing a big operation (*Daily Telegraph*, September 16 2001). The list they provided included the names of four of the 9/11 hijackers, none of whom was arrested ...

'The first hijacking was suspected at not later than 8.20am, and the last hijacked aircraft crashed in Pennsylvania at 10.06 am. Not a single fighter plane was scrambled to investigate from the US Andrews air force base, just 10 miles from Washington DC, until after the third plane had hit the Pentagon at 9.38 am. Why not?

'It is a US legal requirement that once an aircraft has moved significantly off its flight plan, fighter planes are sent up to investigate ... Was this inaction simply the result of key people disregarding, or being ignorant of, the evidence? Or could US air security operations have been deliberately stood down on September 11? If so, why, and on whose authority?

'The former US federal crimes prosecutor, John Loftus, has said: 'The information provided by European intelligence services prior to 9/11 was so extensive that it is no longer possible for either the CIA or FBI to assert a defence of incompetence' ... The overriding motivation for this political smokescreen is that the US and the UK are beginning to run out of secure hydrocarbon energy supplies.

'By 2010 the Muslim world will control as much as 60% of the world's oil production and, even more importantly, 95% of remaining global oil export capacity.'
        — Former British cabinet minister Michael Meacher MP
                    expresses reservations, in *The Guardian*,
                                    6 September 2003

Don't watch my hands (#3)

A picture, in the words of an old advert, tells a thousand words. But what if those words are simply a thousand repetitions of the word 'LIAR' ... or 'LUNATIC' ... or 'INCOMPETENT'?

In days gone by, politicians took their message direct to the people. British Prime Minister William Gladstone, for example, would think nothing of addressing a crowd numbering in the tens of thousands, in the most inclement weather. He knew that his speech would be conveyed to those out of earshot by relay-shouting. Nowadays, politicians have the unadulterated luxury of being able to reach far bigger crowds from a single room. They don't have to rely on whisperers, either. The rise of the print media, and then of the television age, have together meant the advance of something which we might call presentational politics – in terms more familiar to the layman, photo-opportunities. In some ways, this has been a disaster for democracy: politicians are now able to sell you a lie with a beaming smile, flashed live around the world. Those unskilled at putting on a brave face for the cameras are nearly always winnowed out of frontline politics. What politicians have failed to realise is that the camera may be misled, but it never lies. The evidence of their true mental state at the moment the shutter clicks is there for everyone to see – it's just that no one has thought to look for it before.

Human beings, in an ideal situation, are born symmetrical. But only the good Lord himself is perfect, and we are not perfectly symmetrical. For example, most people will readily recognise from everyday experience that they have one eyebrow that sits naturally higher than the other. Try it for yourself. With an observer – better still, with an observer armed with a camera – put your face against the edge of a mirror, so that the reflected half of your face takes the place of the obscured half. Your observer (or the resulting photograph) will be able to tell you that although the resulting composite resembles you, it is as staringly different from you as a police photo-fit would be. In this asymmetry lies the secret of reading politicians' minds.

Pulsing away silently inside your skull, your brain – along with the rest of your body – is divided into two roughly symmetrical halves. These two hemispheres reflect back, mirror-fashion, on to your control of your body: the left hemisphere controls your right hand, right leg and right eye; the right hemisphere controls the left-hand bits. But the important thing here is that the right hemisphere and the left hemisphere work in different ways. The right side of the brain is intuitive, instinctive and deals in analogies. The left brain is rational, logical and analytical.

The left-hand side of the body has had a uniformly bad press for centuries, being associated with the odd, the uncanny and the just plain wrong. Well into the late twentieth century, left-handedness was beaten out of school pupils, who were forced to write with their right. Traditionally, one's guardian angel whispers in the right ear, the devil pours his poison in the left – this is why you throw spilled salt over the left shoulder, to blind the devil (what do you mean, you've never heard of this?). This 'left-evil' connection is even fossilised into the English language – 'sinister' is the Latin for 'left side'. The right hand is your 'dexter' – as in dexterity, the traditional word for skill and ability.

Because the intuitive and instinctive part of the brain controls the left-hand side of the body, the left-hand side of the face tells the truth by accident.

Get hold of pictures of some politicians who are generally agreed to be a bit slippery. (Ideally, these pictures should not be staged 'grip and grin' shots, but should catch the subject at an unrehearsed moment. Being caught with a difficult question during a conference, for example, or confronting an angry rogue member of the public. Needless to say, each of these situations is becoming increasingly rare owing to the rising star of the spin doctors.)

Now, mask off – as precisely as possible – the left-hand side of their face (their left-hand side, that is, not the side that is on the left as you look at it). The remaining side is the half being controlled by the 'conscious' left hemisphere of the brain, or what passes for it, of the politician in question. It will therefore be wearing the expression that the politician is deliberately maintaining, or that he or she is consciously seeking to project in public.

2: Politics by other means

Now mask off the other side of their face. You are – er – left with the left-hand side. This side of the face will usually be wearing a totally different expression. An expression that you might even think looks a little, well ... evil.

While the conscious mind of the politician is struggling to keep up the face expected of it, the unconscious mind is reacting independently and spontaneously to the situation in which it finds itself. Often this will create a 'conflict' situation between the two hemispheres. (They always say serial killers leave clues because they unconsciously want to be caught. Is that so very incomprehensible?) Expressions that you might detect on the left-hand side of a politician's face are panic, horror, a twisted grin, a sneer, or even outright fear, depending on what was going on when the photo was taken. Once you have isolated the two halves, you can put them back together and get the whole story.

- A smiling left but a sneering right? Satisfaction at 'getting away with it' perhaps.
- A stern right but a grinning left? Perhaps you shouldn't take this point too seriously.
- A compassionate right but a panicked left? 'I really need to look as though I care, here.'

This rule-of-thumb method won't work for all politicians, or all of the time. Increasingly, politicians actually believe the words that come out of their own mouths. And sometimes, the two halves will be in perfect harmony because – unimaginably – the person in question will be telling the truth or acting decently. The best subjects for this test are those with a pronounced degree of facial asymmetry, in a difficult situation.

Tony Blair, with his skewed face and heavily asymmetrical eye-balls, was a sitting duck to this method, as was alleged US President George Bush, whose left-hand side usually betrays malice, confusion and uncertainty. On the other hand, archive pictures of Margaret Thatcher looked downright eerie on both halves and the gruff countenance of Gordon Brown seldom registers any mismatch.

An amusing little game to liven up your perusal of the Sunday papers, or the next best thing to a lie detector? Try it and decide among yourselves.

The things they say (#2)

25 September 2002 (press conference, the Oval Office):
The war on terror, you can't distinguish between al Qaeda and Saddam when you talk about the war on terror. And so it's a comparison that is – I can't make because I can't distinguish between the two, because they're both equally as bad, and equally as evil, and equally as destructive.
                    – Alleged US President George W. Bush

31 January 2003 (joint press conference with Blair, White House):
Adam Boulton, Sky News (London) to alleged US President George W. Bush and UK Prime Minister Tony Blair:

> One question for you both. Do you believe that there is a link between Saddam Hussein, a direct link, and the men who attacked on September the 11th?

Bush: I can't make that claim.
Blair: That answers your question.

15 June 2003 (*Meet the Press*, MSNBC):
General Wesley Clark (US Army, ret'd):

> There was a concerted effort during the fall of 2001, starting immediately after 9/11, to pin 9/11 and the terrorism problem on Saddam Hussein.

Tim Russert (host): By who? Who did that?

Clark: Well, it came from the White House, it came from people around the White House. It came from all over. I got a call on 9/11. I was on CNN, and I got a call at my home saying, 'You got to say this is connected. This is state-sponsored terrorism. This has to be connected to Saddam Hussein.' I said, 'But – I'm willing to say it, but what's your evidence?' And I never got any evidence.

14 September 2003 (*Meet the Press*, MSNBC):
We learn more and more that there was a relationship between Iraq and al-Qaeda that stretched back through most of the decade of the '90s, that it involved training, for example, on [biological and chemical weapons], that al-Qaeda sent personnel to Baghdad to get trained on the systems.
— **Alleged US Vice-President Dick Cheney**

7 October 2005 (Presidential press conference, Cincinnati):
We've learned that Iraq has trained al-Qaeda members in bomb-making and poisons and deadly gases.
— **Alleged US President George W. Bush**

'1-888-HARASSU'

For nearly 33 years, sexual harassment has been a crime in the United States. [sound effect: jail door slams] But when a working class woman accused the President of sexual harassment, the clock turned back. The President's men suddenly unleashed a brutal – unsubstantiated attack to discredit the morals and ethics of the woman bringing the charge. No one should be above the law in America – no matter how powerful he is. If you believe you have been a victim of sexual harassment by the President, we want to help.

Call this toll-free number now: 1-888-H-A-R-A-S-S-U.
That's H-A-R-A-S-S-U.
— Commercial aired in November 1997 on radio stations
covering Washington DC, funded by the Free Congress
Foundation (in its first month, the advert
generated more than 4,000 calls)

Oh, say can you see?

New York – The flag raised by three firemen over the
smoldering ruins of the World Trade Center on September
11, 2001 – captured in an iconic image by Thomas
Franklin for *The Record* in Bergen County, New Jersey – is
missing. Actually, it was switched with another flag quite
some time ago – with the media remaining unaware – and
may never be found, writes David Friend in his much-
awaited study of photographs that emerged from that
catastrophe, to be published by Farrar, Strauss and
Giroux in September ...

— News item, 2006

American society is a tribe, 'a civil religion of blood sacrifice,
which periodically kills its children to keep the group together'.

Its god is the flag – a sacred totem which has to be worshipped,
carried, planted and respected: it has the power to doom and
to redeem.

This is the reason that returning troops have to have flags
waved over them – they have survived their intended deaths
and have to be magically 'cleansed' of their stigma in order to
re-enter the society that wanted them dead.

This is not some paranoid pipedream: it is the stone-cold sober
analysis of (American) sociologists Carolyn Marvin and David W.
Ingle of the University of Pennsylvania. Their point is precisely

that this structure is not conscious: it is its unconscious omniscience that gives it power. In their *Blood Sacrifice and the Nation: Totem Rituals and the American Flag* (1999) the authors observe the following.

The Vietnam War was an 'unsuccessful ritual' because it had no clear aims, or victory (or, indeed, end), and the surviving 'sacrifices' were not ritually absorbed back into the group. The result has been a wound in American life that refuses to heal.

Presidential elections are a symbolic mating ritual in which the population chooses a fertile partner to 'rejuvenate' the country. This is the real reason why President Clinton was impeached on what appeared to be a private and personal matter of marital infidelity.

The real taboo against flag-burning is nothing to do with patriotism as such: it is actually the physical destruction of the tribe's fetish. Similar taboos exist in the US's domestic flag-making industry, in which surplus reels of uncut flags must be destroyed under supervised conditions or else neutralised by being dyed black, then shredded and sold as stuffing.

Ingle and Marvin report a major scandal that never made the news outside the US because it is meaningless to the rest of the world: *undyed but mutilated flags found in the stuffing of Asian sofas imported to the United States!*

Chuck your passport (#2)

How would you empty an island? Without getting caught, I mean? And without killing anyone? In the 1960s, Britain did exactly this, to the Indian Ocean island of Diego Garcia. Diego Garcia – part of the British Indian Ocean Territories (BIOT) – was inhabited by some 2,000 people, who worked on privately owned plantations. The nearest neighbours to this tropical idyll were on Mauritius, some 1,900 kilometres (1,200 miles) to the west, which the Diego Garcians occasionally visited to spend their wages (even though the round trip took months, including waiting for a ship home).

But there was trouble brewing for this simple paradise. America was in search of a 'secure communications facility' in the Indian Ocean. Lured by the smell of Big Dollars (to say nothing of a diplomatic solution to its nuclear defence problems), Britain decided to trick the Diego Garcians into leaving. In April 1967, Britain bought all the plantations of the Chagos archipelago for £660,000 from the Chagos Agalega Company and quietly began closing them down.

Colonial Office head Denis Greenhill (later Lord Greenhill of Harrow) wrote to the British Delegation at the UN:

> The object of the exercise is to get some rocks which will remain ours; there will be no indigenous population except seagulls who have not yet got a committee. Unfortunately, along with the seagulls go a few Tarzans and Man Fridays who are hopefully being wished on Mauritius.

Another internal Colonial Office memo read:

> The Colonial Office ... wish to avoid using the phrase 'permanent inhabitants' in relation to any of the islands in the territory because to recognise that there are any permanent inhabitants will imply that there is a population whose democratic rights will have to be safeguarded and which will therefore be deemed by the UN to come within its purlieu. The solution proposed is to issue them with documents making it clear that they are 'belongers' of Mauritius and the Seychelles and only temporary residents of BIOT. This device, although rather transparent, would at least give us a defensible position to take up at the UN.

Starting in March 1969, Diego Garcians taking a break on Mauritius found that they were no longer allowed to get on the steamer home. They were told their contracts to work on Diego Garcia had expired. This left them homeless, jobless and without means of support. It also prevented word from reaching the rest of the Diego Garcia population. Relatives who travelled to Mauritius to investigate their missing family members also found themselves unable to return.

In March 1971, the US Navy arrived and began setting up shop. In October that year, the last remaining Diego Garcians held a mass in the island's church and put down their donkeys. Their dogs were rounded up and gassed and the Garcians were shipped off the island. The last stragglers were dumped with their abandoned relatives on Mauritius, where most had already begun the slide into petty crime, prostitution, drink, despair and frequent suicide.

On 11 May 2006 the British High Court ruled that the Diego Garcians were entitled to return. There is still not the slightest sign of this happening. The US lease comes up for renegotiation in 2016 – at which point a further fifty-year lease is expected. The sign at the heavily guarded harbour of the 'austere communications facility' of Diego Garcia reads: 'Welcome to the footprint of freedom.'

It couldn't happen here

In 1965, the British government finally drowned the Welsh village of Capel Celyn, one of the last Welsh-speaking villages left in the Principality.

On 27 January 1961, the last steam train chugged out of Cym Tryweryn station, carrying the village's last-remaining inhabitants.

Sixty-seven Welsh-speaking families who had lived in Capel Celyn for hundreds of years were uprooted.

Their homes were flooded, along with the post office, the Methodist and Calvinist chapels, acres of farmland and over a hundred cottages.

The flooding was the result of the damming of the river Dee, as ordered by the government's 1957 Tryweryn Bill, which was designed to alleviate the water supply problems facing the city of Liverpool.

Welsh people saw this as England's deliberate destruction of Welsh culture in order to supply the occupying nation with water.

Thirty-five out of Wales's thirty-six MPs opposed the Tryweryn Bill – but it was passed anyway.

An eight-year attempt by the valley community to prevent the destruction of their homes came to an end in 1965, when the village, with its post office, school, chapels and cemetery slid beneath the waves.

3: Towards the hive planet

Do not fold, spindle or mutilate.
— Slogan chanted by University of California
students, protesting at IBM punch card
registration methods, 1964

There is a time when the operation of the machine becomes so odious, makes you so sick at heart, that you can't take part; and you've got to put your bodies upon the wheels, upon the levers, upon all the apparatus and you've got to make it stop. And you've got to indicate to the people who run it, to the people who own it, that unless you're free, the machine will be prevented from working at all.
— Mario Savio, student activist, California,
2 December 1964, shortly before the arrest
of 800 fellow demonstrators

If I point out that General Motors tries to maximise profits and market share, that's not a conspiracy theory, that's an institutional analysis.
— Noam Chomsky

The fossil-powered dream world of tomorrow

The Year of Grace, 1942 – I am standing on Shakspere's Cliff, or what remains of it, wondering at the ruins of the railroad, and waiting for the daily post from Australasia. I see a speck in the clouds, and hail the harbinger of news. The postman alights for half-a-second (his regulation breathing time), folds his caoutchouc wings, sucks

99

in a concentrated lozenge the virtues of a quart of London porter, blows his nose with an asbestos pocket handkerchief, and is off again like a rocket, before I have seen whether my letters have the postmark of Adelaide or of Sydney.
— 'A Glance Into The Future', *Ainsworth's Magazine*, **Summer 1842**

The eighteenth century arrived, and with it James Watt. The brain of that man was the spore out of which was developed the modern steam-engine, and all the prodigious trees and branches of modern industry which have grown out of this. But coal is as much an essential condition of this growth and development as carbonic acid is for that of a club-moss. Wanting coal, we could not have smelted the iron needed to make our engines, nor have worked our engines when we had got them. But take away the engines, and the great towns of Yorkshire and Lancashire vanish like a dream. Manufacturers give place to agriculture and pasture, and not ten men can live where now ten thousand are amply supported.
— **Thomas Huxley, 'Discourses', 1894**

The idea of an earthly paradise in which men should live together in a state of brotherhood, without laws and without brute labour, had haunted the human imagination for thousands of years. And this vision had had a certain hold even on the groups who actually profited by each historical change. The heirs of the French, English, and American revolutions had partly believed in their own phrases about the rights of man, freedom of speech, equality before the law, and the like, and had even allowed their conduct to be influenced by them to some extent. But ... [the] earthly paradise had been discredited at exactly the moment when it became realizable.

Every new political theory, by whatever name it called itself, led back to hierarchy and regimentation. And in the general hardening of outlook ... practices which had been long abandoned, in some cases for hundreds of years – imprisonment without trial, the use of war prisoners as slaves, public executions, torture to extract confessions, the use of hostages, and the deportation of whole populations – not only became common again, but were tolerated and even defended by people who considered themselves enlightened and progressive.'
— Emmanuel Goldstein, *The Theory and Practice of Oligarchical Collectivism*, 1984

Computers vote Bush

Where the result of an election has been in dispute, the traditional response has been to recount the votes. But what do you do when there's nothing to recount?

That was the situation that faced Florida voters in early 2004. A seat in the House of Representatives had been won by 12 votes, but the electronic voting system that had recently been installed had registered 127 blank votes. In an Indiana election the year before, an electronic system registered 144,000 votes in an election with fewer than 19,000 registered voters.

Horror stories such as these inspired David Dill, professor of computer science at Stanford University, to call for a 'paper trail' so that electronic voting could be double-checked. Some 1,600 technicians and fifty elected officials had backed his call.

Speaking to the American Association for the Advancement of Science in February 2004, Dill said; 'The system is in crisis. A quarter of the American public is voting on machines where there's very little protection for their votes. If the machine silently changes or loses the vote, the voter has no clue what has happened. I don't think there's any reason to trust these machines.' Nine months later, America went to the polls to elect a president, whom all the opinion polls indicated would, by a comfortable margin, be John Kerry. Still stinging from the 2000 debacle, in which Bush was appointed president by the Supreme Court after a protracted recount was halted, the media relied heavily on exit polls to gauge the election's progress.

An exit poll is one in which voters leaving the polling booth are asked which way they voted, thus giving a tight match with the actual voting pattern, rather than relying on the reported intentions of voters (as in a pre-vote poll). The exit polls indicated a Kerry victory. When the result came in, Bush had won.

Former Clinton aide Dick Morris sneered: 'The networks got the exit polls wrong. Not just some of them. They got all of the Bush states wrong. To screw up one exit poll is unheard of. To miss six of them is incredible.'

Referring to the fact that different US time zones mean early results can be known before polling in other areas has closed, he added: 'The possibility of biased exit polling, deliberately manipulated to try to dishearten the Bush turnout, must be seriously considered. Exit pollsters should have to explain, in public, how they were so wrong.'

The electronic voting machines themselves declined to comment.

'I've Been Murdered'

In their relentless persecution of Germany's Jews, gypsies and homosexuals, the Nazis benefited from the world's leading computer manufacturer.

In the 1930s, US information technology giants International Business Machines (IBM) entered into agreements to provide a punch-card database of Germany's inhabitants.

IBM's technology was used during censuses, registration and ancestral tracing programmes to weed out Germany's Jewish inhabitants. Once the Jews had been identified, IBM's billion-card scheme helped plan the railway schedules that took the Jews to the extermination camps and provided work programmes once they were there.

Thanks to the six-position rows of identifiers on each identification card, each German concentration camp could potentially register and track 999,999 inmates.

The system was also introduced to occupied countries under the guise of an 'audit' by their conquerors. In occupied France, the *New York Times* reported in 1941: 'Special registering machines are being used in this census. By a system of perforations, every citizen will receive a number composed of thirteen digits. Information will be obtainable county by county.'

Writer Edwin Black, who uncovered this forgotten area of computer history wrote:

> Many of us have become enraptured in the Age of Computerisation and the Age of Information. I know I have. But now I am consumed with a new awareness that for me, as the son of Holocaust survivors, brings me to a whole new consciousness.
>
> I call it the Age of Realisation, as we look back and examine technology's wake. Unless we understand how the Nazis acquired the names, more lists will be compiled against more people.

Dang An

For nearly fifty years, China has held a personal dossier on every single one of its billion citizens. This file is called a Dang

An (also 'dang'an' and variations) and is a lifelong personnel file exposing your intimate life history from birth onwards.

You are never allowed to see it and you don't know what it contains. Nobody can work in China without a Dang An.

In the words of Chinese national Jian Shuo Wang:

> [Dang An] can be translated to 'Personal History Documents' or 'Personal Credit Documents' ... Everyone has a copy of big brown envolop. It starts from very early (in primary school?). All the documents about the person are kept in this brown envolop. If you committed criminal or bad things, it will be recorded as one document in the envolop. What is interesting though, is that anyone are not allowed to see his/her own Dang'an. I don't know what is in it for me. I just know I have to transfer to Dang'an into my university, and transfer it to FESCO after graduate. I never saw anyone else's Dang'an. I saw the envolop once, I believe. It is always a misterious for me.

In the words of one BBC correspondent:

> A black mark against you – a bad school report, a disagreement with your boss, a visit to a psychiatrist – all can travel with you for the rest of your life. One person I know once caught a glimpse of her Dang An. In it was a pink slip of paper she recognised as coming from her primary school. Things she had done as an eight-year-old child are still following her more than 20 years later.

On 5 August 2002, the Japanese government introduced its Juki Net (resident registry). Every single one of Japan's 126 million citizens is now tagged with an eleven-digit identification number, which acts as a unique identifier. The code number allows files to be accessed and cross-referenced by civil servants in every area of Japanese life. Information catalogued includes name, age, gender, date of birth, addresses, criminal records and health data.

Prior to its introduction, Hirohisha Kitano, Professor Emeritus at Nihon University said: 'The Nazis assigned numbers to people in exactly the same way. It's extremely dangerous.' The Mayor of Tokyo's Suganami district said: 'The government is acting illegally because it is launching this database without there being laws to protect personal information.' Opinion polls found that 80 per cent of Japanese people were opposed to the database.

But it's far too late now.

34,310: the number of passports 'lost' by the British Government in 2001–2006

(20,660 passports returned to licence applicants by the Driver and Vehicle Licensing Agency plus 13,650 new documents issued by the UK Passport Service)

250,000: the number of British people who disappear each year

Of these, 175,000 will turn up again within three days and 25,000 will be found dead. The remaining 50,000 are never found.

According to the National Missing Persons Helpline, men are twice as likely to disappear as women. The typical 'vanisher' will be an outwardly confident adult, masking secret feelings of disappointment and frustration. He needs to be practical enough to organise a convincingly faked death.

'Suicide' is obviously the most popular option, as per John Stonehouse, the MP who left his clothes on a beach in the mid-1970s and turned up alive and well in Australia. But a large-scale disaster will do just as well as a cover story, provided you can pull it off.

Former sex offender Karl Hackett had disappeared in 1980 and was living under the alias Lee Simm when he decided to 'kill off' his old identity in the Paddington rail disaster of October 1999 (this obviously didn't work, or you wouldn't be reading about him – he was nicked for wasting police time).

The other vital preparation is money. The NMPH estimates that a would-be vanisher needs about £16,000 to cover documentation, travel and accommodation.

'Hundreds of thousands': the number of personal details stolen by civil servants

An internal investigation of the British government's Department for Work and Pensions (DWP) found that civil servants are working with organised crime and stealing hundreds of thousands of sets of personal details.

The DWP's databases store details such as national insurance numbers, names, addresses and social security details. With these, you can commit benefit fraud, set up false bank accounts and obtain official documents such as passports. The ID theft from DWP and Revenue and Customs databases is currently the subject of an internal investigation, codenamed Trident, carried out in conjunction with the government's official data-protection watchdog. One 'government figure' told the British press: 'We have been told that DWP staff have been colluding with organised criminals to commit identity theft on an industrial scale. It is far wider than just tax credits and reaches right across Whitehall.'

The Information Commissioner, Richard Thomas, told the *Independent on Sunday* that there are 'widespread concerns' that poorly paid staff in tax and benefits offices are 'open to temptation'.

1,000,000: people invented by the Office of National Statistics

During the ten-yearly census of UK residents in 2001, 2 per cent of the UK population was missed by the clipboard-wielding bureaucrats.

The Office of National Statistics (ONS) therefore invented them. Census-takers added in more twenty-something males, eighty-something women, pre-school children, non-English speakers and flat-dwellers. Professor Paul Boyle of St Andrews University, who was consulted by the ONS on the technique, said: 'We have every reason to believe this produces a more accurate picture of the UK population.' Which may be true, but he didn't say what he was comparing it to.

Still, inventing a million people must go some way towards cancelling out the supposed scale of identity theft (or 'fraud', as we used to call it).

Speaking of which ...

'Everyone': the proportion of UK Citizens who are intended to end up carrying the British identity card

The question 'Why?' is not one that the British government has found easy to answer in a straightforward manner.

Multiple or false identities are used in more than a third of terrorist-related activity and in organised crime and money laundering.

It is crucial we are able robustly to ascertain and verify our own and others' identities. The public understand this and there is widespread support for an ID cards scheme. There has been a growing recognition that, rather than threatening our vital freedoms, ID cards would actually help preserve them.'
— **David Blunkett MP, British Home Secretary, 26 April 2004**

The question on ID cards, but also on any other security measure actually, is on the balance of the ability to deal with particular threats and civil liberties, does a particular measure help or hinder it? I actually think ID cards do help rather than hinder. If you ask me whether ID cards or any other measure would have stopped [the bombing of the London Underground] yesterday, I can't identify any measure which would have just stopped it like that.
— **Charles Clarke MP, British Home Secretary, 8 July 2005**

I want to make it very clear to the public that this draft Bill is not just about an ID card, but an extensive National Identity Register (NIR) and the creation of a National Identity Registration Number (NIRN). Each of these raise substantial data protection and personal privacy concerns in their own right. Further clarification is also needed [for] the reasons why such a large amount of information needs to be recorded as part of establishing an individual's identity. I also have concerns in relation to the wide range of bodies who can view the record of what services individuals have used. This will enable the Government and others to

build up a comprehensive picture of how we live our lives. However, individuals will not know which bodies have been accessing their personal information.
— **Richard Thomas, British Information Commissioner, 30 July 2004**

If we have ID cards at vast expense and people can go into a back room and forge them they are going to be absolutely useless. ID cards may be helpful in all kinds of things but I don't think they are necessarily going to make us any safer.
— **Dame Stella Rimington, former MI5 chief, 17 November 2005**

There is no way you're going to be able to track people who are in this country without identity cards.
— **Tony Blair, British Prime Minister, 16 July 2006**

'A generation': the possible delay to the introduction of British ID cards that may be caused by the Blair government's over-eager attempt to introduce them.

In December 2006, it was announced that the National Identity Register would no longer be one giant database, but would be held on three separate pre-existing Home Office systems, one of which will be the asylum seeker database. The 'Labour' Party's enthusiasm for gigantic IT systems is frightening, but all the more so when you consider that the prime minister who led the way on ID cards has openly confessed to not being able to work a computer. By the time you read this, further wheels may have fallen off the project. This may seem heartening, but don't think the ID card system is going away.

To judge by the emailed words of Home Office civil servants, as leaked to *The Times*, the ballsing-up of the current ID card plan may delay what is apparently just part of a longer-term vision for Britain:

> I do not have a problem with ministers wanting a face-saving solution, but we need to be clear with the programme team, senior officials, special advisors and ministers etc. just what this implies. They need to understand this, because a botched introduction of a descoped early variant ID Card backed by TNIR, if it is subject to a media feeding frenzy (queues outside passport offices! and more recently IND) – which it might well be close to a general election, could put back the introduction of ID Cards for a generation and won't do much for IPS credibility nor for the Govt's election chances either (latter not our problem but might play with ministers).

In normal everyday English, putting something back by a generation means you'll never do it because you'll be too old or dead. But in the words of David Owen: "Governments come and go, the civil service goes on forever." A generation is nothing to the state.

Information to be included on the British ID card and National Identity Register, as set out in the ID Card Act 2005

Full name
Other names by which bearer has been known
Date of birth
Place of birth
Gender
Principal UK place of residence
Every other UK place of residence
Past places of UK and overseas residence 'during a
    prescribed period'
Head and shoulders photograph

Signature

Fingerprints

'Other biometric information'

Residential status

Nationality

Entitlement to remain in the United Kingdom

The terms and conditions of leave to enter or remain in
   the UK, if applicable

'Personal reference numbers etc.'

National Identity Registration Number

Number of any ID card issued

Any national insurance number

Number of any immigration document

Number of any United Kingdom passport

Number of any non-UK passport

Number of any document that can be used instead of a
   passport

Number of any overseas identity card

Any reference number in connection with an application to
   enter or to remain in the UK

Number of any work permit

Number of any driving licence

'The number of any other designated document'

The date of expiry or period of validity of a document listed
   above

Previous records of the above information

Changes affecting the above information and changes
   made to the Register entry

'Date of death.'

The date of every application for registration

The date of every application for a modification of the
   registry entry

The date of every application confirming the contents of
   the registry entry

The reason for any omission from the information recorded

Particulars (in addition to its number) of every ID card issued

Whether each such card is in force and, if not, why not

Particulars of every person who has countersigned an application

Particulars of every notification given by him (lost, stolen and damaged cards, etc.)

Particulars of every requirement to surrender an ID card

The information provided in connection with every application or modification

The information provided in connection with every registry entry confirmation

The steps taken to identify the applicant or verify the information provided

Any other steps or information used to ensure a complete, up-to-date, accurate entry

Particulars of every notification given by that individual.

A PIN used in connection with applications or information provision

A password used for the above purpose

Questions and answers to be used for security when applying or modifying information.

Particulars of every occasion on which the registry entry has been accessed

Particulars of every person to whom such information has been provided

Other particulars associated with the registry access

Information to be included on the American ID card introduced under the Real ID Act 2005

The land of the brave and the home of the free is set to get something very similar to Britain's ID Card system. 'Real ID' (as opposed to every other form of pre-existing ID) will include the following (pay particular attention to the euphemistic last category):

Bearer's full legal name
Date of birth
Gender

Driver's license or identification card number
Digital photograph of the bearer's face
Bearer's address of principal residence.
Bearer's signature
'Physical security features designed to prevent tampering,
    counterfeiting, or duplication of the document for
    fraudulent purposes'

The Real ID is vital to preventing foreign terrorists from
hiding in plain sight while conducting their operations
and planning attacks. By targeting terrorist travel, the
Real ID will assist in our war-on-terror efforts to disrupt
terrorist operations and help secure our borders.
— **Rep. F. James Sensenbrenner, Wisconsin (Republican),**
House of Representatives, 10 May 2005

The Real ID Act will protect the American people by
allowing immigration judges to determine witness credi-
bility in asylum cases and ensuring that all terrorism-
related grounds for inadmissibility are also grounds for
deportation.
— **Rep. Charles W. Pickering, Mississippi (Republican),**
House of Representatives, 10 February 2005

'Britain will become the first police state in the democratic world'

— **the biggest fear of former Prime Minister Sir Edward**
Heath, one year after leaving office in 1974,
according to a BBC TV reporter.

The one-way street of surveillance ...

Britain's Freedom of Information Act (FOIA) was passed into
law in 2000 but didn't take effect until 2005, during which

113

time hundreds of thousands of sensitive files were pre-emptively shredded.

The Department of Trade and Industry destroyed 52,605 files in 1999–2000, but 97,020 in 2003–2004.

The Ministry of Defence didn't keep track of the number of files it destroyed but (with typical military mentality) did record that it had shredded 4,618 'linear metres' of documents. Since then, the Ministry of Defence has also claimed that some 63,000 files, containing around 10 million pages, are no longer accessible to FOIA requests, having been contaminated with asbestos while in storage. These documents included files with titles such as 'Sale of Arms to Saudi Arabia', 'Production of Chemical Weapons' and 'Medical Aspects of Interrogation'. Other files bear the evocative titles 'Operation Tiara', 'Operation Grape' and 'Project R1'.

Under FOIA anyone has the right to request access to information held by government departments and agencies. This includes written files, reports, directories and memos, electronic data such as the contents of emails and databases; and other forms of data such as photographs and films.

All you have to do is make a written request to the authority you believe holds the information you are after. They then have twenty working days to reply, or you can complain to the Information Commissioner's Office. You can complain to the holding authority if you believe that their answer is incorrect, and complain to the Information Commissioner if you are still not satisfied after that.

However, statutory exemptions to FOIA mean material may be withheld in whole or part under the following clauses of the Act:

Section 21: Information accessible by other means

3: Towards the hive planet

Section 22: Information intended for future publication
Section 23: Information supplied by, or related to, bodies
dealing with security matters
Section 24: National security
Section 26: Defence
Section 27: International relations
Section 28: Relations within the United Kingdom
Section 29: The economy
Section 30: Investigations and proceedings conducted by
public authorities
Section 31: Law enforcement
Section 32: Court records
Section 33: Audit functions
Section 34: Parliamentary privilege
Section 35: Formulation of government policy
Section 36: Prejudice to effective conduct of public affairs
Section 37: Communications with Her Majesty, with other
members of the Royal Household, and the
conferring by the Crown of any honour or
dignity
Section 38: Health and safety
Section 39: Environmental information
Section 40: Personal information
Section 41: Information provided in confidence
Section 42: Legal professional privilege
Section 43: Commercial interests
Section 44: Prohibitions on disclosure

You will note that FOIA does not cover anything that is not already recorded. Which is why more and more civil servants and politicians are using off-the-record means of communication – such as phone calls, informal chats and discussions round the office water cooler. (This was one of the key criticisms in Lord Butler's 2004 inquiry into whether the government had lied over Iraq's alleged weapons of mass destruction. Key decision-making meetings and policy formulations were held in Blair's 'sofa cabinet' – an informal and totally unrecorded forum in which ministers and officials sat around in their shirtsleeves, drinking tea and formulating the warping of intelligence reports in the same breezy way that you or I might discuss a forthcoming shopping trip.)

Meanwhile, British citizens are the most spied-upon in the world ... according to the Information Commissioner himself. The cross-referencing of databases and surveillance systems means people are now having their movements tracked routinely while going about their daily lives.

Britain now has 4,200,000 public CCTV cameras – roughly one camera for every fourteen people. The average Briton will be filmed by CCTV around 300 times every day. Automatic number plate recognition cameras are used to track people's road journeys (despite never having been made legal).

The Regulation of Investigatory Powers Act 2000 means that domestic Internet histories can be intercepted under the control of the police, the armed forces, nine government departments and 'any local authority'.

In 2004, it was revealed that the Department of Trade and Industry and the Department for Work and Pensions planned to secretly monitor phone calls from the public for signs of vocal stress that might betray fraudulent benefit and compensation claimants.

Information Commissioner Richard Thomas told *The Times*: 'People are being scrutinised and having their lives tracked, and are not even aware of it. They don't know, for instance, that a record is kept of every internet site they visit.'

Thomas added: 'They don't realise that when identity cards come in, there will be a record of their movements and every time they have engaged with any public service.'

3: Towards the hive planet

The Commissioner's views on ID cards and the National Identity Register have been set out very concisely in a report that has been totally ignored. Thomas wrote:

> The government has made clear that the system of operation it favours involves checks by service providers back to the National Identity Register thus building up a picture of an individual's card use and a detailed picture from this of how they live their lives. The creation of this detailed data trail of individuals' activities is particularly worrying and cannot be viewed in isolation from other initiatives which serve to build a detailed picture of people's lives. Each development puts in place another component in the infrastructure of a 'surveillance society'. If we are to have an identity card, the Information Commissioner would like it to be a tool to assist individuals to demonstrate their identity when they find it useful. It should be a tool within the individual's control. The primary aim of government with this legislation should be to establish a scheme which allows people to reliably identify themselves rather than one which enhances its ability to identify and record what its citizens do in their lives.

Where is the demand for scrutiny of the people who will be monitoring your life?

The best you can get is restricted access to some permanent records kept by government – and you can't even know what those records are in advance of asking whether they exist. There is currently no movement to install webcams in civil service departments. Nor to routinely record their phone calls, so that you can know what was said 'off the record' concerning anything they deal with. Politicians can make decisions outside meetings – and there is no way of knowing about it, no record left and no way of proving wrongdoing.

You elect politicians, from parish councillors to prime ministers.

Your taxes pay the wages of the civil servants who monitor you. And you have no way of keeping track of them. Nor, if they have their way, will you. Ever.

Prints of darkness

Brandon Mayfield is a lucky man. The Portland lawyer's finger-prints were found at the crime scene of one of the 11 March 2004 Madrid bombings. Three FBI examiners agreed the print was his. But it wasn't. Islamic convert Mayfield spent seventeen days in detention after the FBI Lab wrongly linked him to prints recovered by Spanish police from plastic bags that contained detonator caps.

In a public statement, the FBI said:

> The FBI identification was based on an image of substandard quality, which was particularly problematic because of the remarkable number of points of similarity between Mayfield's prints and the print details in the images submitted to the FBI. The FBI's Latent Fingerprint Unit will be reviewing its current practices and will give consideration to adopting new guidelines for all exam-iners receiving latent print images when the original evidence is not included.

This impressive-sounding statement may seem to imply that an immediate review of fingerprint science is being carried out. But it isn't – not least because fingerprint identification is not a science in the first place.

Fingerprinting has never been scientifically validated as an identification method, for the obvious reason that its error rate is impossible to determine without fingerprinting everyone in the whole world for comparison purposes.

There is thus no foolproof way of proving that one fingerprint is the same as another or that it couldn't come from a different person. (You may have noticed that the police employ people whose job it is to come up with an illustration resembling the face of a suspect they wish to trace. These people are called 'police artists', not 'face scientists'.) Certified fingerprint experts, using no equipment apart from their eyes and brains, look for corresponding points between two prints – a 'found' print (that is, one retrieved from a crime scene) and an 'obtained' print (got by inking a suspect). Once they've found a certain number of matches, they have something they can enter into evidence before a court, stating that they believe they have found a match. The number of matches required depends on the standard of probability accepted by the legal system of whichever country happens to be trying you.

Studies of error rates in fingerprinting indicate that the rate of false matches in America alone averages around 1 per cent a year. Which may not seem like much, but works out at some 2,000 people wrongly – er – fingered each year.

Fingerprints don't convict people – people convict people.

In a British study by Itiel Dror and Ailsa Peron of the University of Southampton in 2005, fingerprint experts were fooled into repudiating matches to which they had previously testified in court. They were given 'found' prints and 'obtained' prints and asked to check the correspondences between the two. But they were also told, in passing, that the two prints were the same prints that had been entered into evidence in the well-publicised case of Brandon Mayfield the previous year.

The researchers called this the 'top-down' effect, because the aim was to see whether the print experts would be influenced by extra information from someone supposedly better informed than them.

'Knowing' in advance that the prints shouldn't match, three out of five fingerprint examiners found that there was no match between the found print and the suspect's provided print. A fourth said there was insufficient information in the prints to either match or mismatch. In fact, each examiner had been given a different set of prints – ones that they had themselves presented in court as definite matches five years earlier. (The thoughts of the fifth examiner – who found himself believing he had in fact found an unexpected match in something he knew to be a famous legal near-miss – can only be imagined.)

Dror and Peron concluded:

> Our findings need to be examined within the context of routine everyday work of fingerprint experts. The training, experience, and work procedures of fingerprint experts may play an interesting and crucial role in if and how top-down components play a role in fingerprint identification.

> On the one hand, fingerprint experts may be less susceptible to top-down interference, perhaps even immune to such effects. Given their highly specialized skills, they may be able to focus solely on the bottom-up component and be data driven without the external influences that we have observed in the research reported here.

> On the other hand, and in contrast, fingerprint experts may be even more susceptible to such top-down components. Their vast knowledge and experience may provide them with extra degrees of freedom to rationalize and justify what they are biased to find.

Computerised recognition systems may be less susceptible to persuasion, but they are far more open to other pitfalls. And because there's no way of error-checking their verdicts without human review, it means that biometric recognition systems are wide open to being fooled.

One amateur has led the way by experimenting with a mixture of one part gelatine to one part water, which naturally regains its original shape unless fixed by cooling. By taking a cast of his own finger and popping it in the freezer to set, he was able to fool a scanner into accepting a bubble-filled 'false' print more than half the time.

Another experimenter has found an even better way to 'lift' an original fingerprint for your own use.

First, you make the print visible, using powdered graphite or superglue. Then you photograph it and scan it into your computer. There, you use a standard art package to remove flaws in the photographed print (filling in any little gaps or bubbles and making sure ridges are continuous). You then print it off, life-size, on to a transparency and cover it with household wood glue. The toner powder on the transparency is microscopically raised above its surface – but even this is enough to produce usable impressions in the glue, varying in depth corresponding to the ridges of the print. Leave it to set, and the print transfers itself to the rubbery wood glue in full 3-D glory. The print can then be cut to size, wrapped around your fingertip and stuck into place.

How reliable are these home-made dabs? The answer is: between 68 and 100 per cent of the time.

In 2002, Tsutomu Matsumoto of Yokohama National University led a research team that tricked fingerprint scanners with false fingers made of gelatine. Using methods no less basic than the ones described above, gelatine was found to be the best medium for a 'gummy' (that is, fake) because, like skin, it conducts quite well (unlike materials such as putty), thus fooling even scanners with 'live and well' sensors – especially when the 'gummy' was wetted with saliva.

Matsumoto found:

> There are many ways to deceive fingerprint recognition systems, even if their templates and communication are protected by security measures.
>
> For example, gelatine and soft plastic materials are easy to obtain at grocery stores and hobby shops. The fact that 'gummy' fingers are easy to make with cheap, easily obtained, tools and materials, suggests reviews not only of fingerprint systems but also of biometric systems. The experimental study on gummy fingers will have considerable impact on the security assessments of fingerprint systems.

So far, Matsumoto's optimistic prediction has not been fulfilled.

100,000: the approximate number of UK citizens who have wrongfully been swabbed and added to the UK's National DNA database

These people – equivalent to the entire population of Crawley in Sussex – were forced to give a genetic sample despite never being warned, cautioned, charged or convicted in connection with any offence. When this was revealed in 2006, the Home Office said: 'It's not a criminal database. It's an intelligence base.'

425,033: the approximate number of black UK residents on the database

This is 37 per cent of the total black population and roughly the equivalent of the entire population of Bristol.

600,000: the number of British people convicted of crimes on the basis of DNA evidence between 1999 and summer 2006

750,000: the number of ten- to seventeen-year-olds added to the database for things such as committing a crime, being suspected of committing a crime, witnessing a crime, being a victim of crime or riding a bike on the pavement

This figure is equivalent to somewhere between the population of Glasgow (629,000 according to the 2001 Census) and Birmingham (970,000)

3,500,000: the number of people on the database in mid-2006, according to police

4,500,000: the number of people who will be on the database by mid-2008

'Everyone': the number of UK residents that Prime Minister Tony Blair claimed should be put on the register

311: the number of serious offences in Britain (murder, attempted murder and sex offences) between 2001 and 2005 matched to DNA from previously released suspects

- DNA that would have been removed from the database had the law not been altered in 2001 to allow its retention.

123

10,443: the number of other offences in Britain that were matched by the same method, but *weren't* murder, attempted murder, rape or sex offences

The Home Office estimates that of the DNA profiles that would previously have been removed, 7,591 profiles of individuals have been matched to 10,754 offences, including 88 murders, 45 attempted murders, 116 rapes and 62 sexual offences. (Please note that 'matched to' does not – or should not – mean 'convicted of'.)

1:37,000,000: the impressive-sounding odds against a burglary suspect being wrongly matched to DNA found at a British crime scene in February 2000

Suspect Raymond Easton had advanced Parkinson's disease, couldn't walk, could barely dress himself, had no driving licence, lived more than 200 miles from the crime scene and had an alibi from a family member. His DNA had ended up on the national database some time before, when he was arrested (and released without charge) after hitting his daughter during a family row.

DNA is the material that dictates the inheritance of physical characteristics such as hair colour, stature, eye colour, facial features, hair patterns, bone density and just about everything else that makes you like your parents. Each DNA molecule is about 30 centimetres (1 foot) long, but is so thin that it can be packed into a space of less than a fiftieth of a cubic millimetre. It's found in just about every cell of the human body (except red blood cells – human blood can only be tested for DNA because of the presence of white blood cells).

It's composed of just four proteins, referred to by their initials – C, T, G and A – occurring in an apparently random sequence millions of times. The precise ways that 'crime scene' DNA is tested for matches with a suspect's DNA are probably far beyond those of us without a scientific background. Fortunately, these methods are also irrelevant here.

Without going into technical detail, forensic DNA scientists look for matches between what are called 'loci' – given sections along DNA molecules. In the case cited above, six loci were found to match between suspect and crime-scene sample. But – as was found when his solicitor demanded a retest, looking for more loci – another four loci from our disabled 'burglar' did not match the crime scene DNA. Mr Easton was released without apology and the Crown Prosecution Service sent him a letter which stated that charges were being dropped 'because there is not enough evidence to provide a realistic chance of conviction'.

But with odds of one in 37,000,000 against a false match, how did this man get wrongly identified? The answer lies precisely in those impressive-looking odds themselves. Professor Andre Moenssens interviewed over a hundred British judges about the case and found that every single one believed that the odds meant the defendant's DNA pattern would only occur once in a sample of 37,000,000 people.

Given the enormous correspondence between individuals' DNA patterns (we are, after all, only human), those odds actually mean that a similar six-loci match could occur between dozens of people out of a sample of just 700,000 subjects. The 1:37,000,000 figure is the result of a mathematical fallacy, caused by using the 'productive rule' and multiplying up the chances of a match at each by the number of loci being examined. If the chance of one match at one loci is 1:10, it stands to reason that the chances of matches at 13 loci are 1: (10 x 10 x 10 x 10 x 10 x 10 x 10 x 10 x 10 x 10 x 10 x 10 x 10) – or one in ten billion (10,000,000,000,000). This is beyond any level of reliability ever achieved by anything, and is probably greater even than the odds against the sun not coming up tomorrow.

The 1:10,000,000,000,000 mind-boggler only refers to the odds of getting the same result by chance *in thirteen independent experiments involving one locus* – not of finding matches at thirteen points in a given string of essentially random (but pre-determined) information.

No one knows what the real odds against a false DNA 'match' are.

To date, there has been just one experiment to find out how likely you really are to find random matches from a given number of samples. A 2005 study of the Arizona CODIS database – which contained a mere 65,493 entries – showed that approximately one in every 228 profiles in the database matched another profile in the database at nine or more loci.

- One in every 1,489 profiles matched at 10 loci.
- One in 16,374 profiles matched at 11 loci.
- One in 32,747 matched at 12 loci.

But thanks to the wide-eyed amazement with which DNA evidence is treated by laymen (judges, juries and journalists alike), a DNA match has become commonly accepted as a proof of guilt more damning than being caught red-handed with a smoking gun. So much so that the American professor who first called attention to the Arizona CODIS results received correspondence that:

> seemed (I'm being generous with this wording) to suggest that my goal was to help dangerous criminals escape conviction and continue to do harm to innocent citizens. I find it impossible to get inside the mind of a citizen of a country based on what is to my mind the most impres-

sive founding documents the world has ever seen (I refer to the Declaration of Independence, the US Constitution, and the Bill of Rights) who reads my words as anything but a sincere plea that we adhere to the principles set out in those documents. Consequently, I have no idea what I could say that would convince such a person otherwise.

Which was precisely the situation in which Raymond Easton found himself. But that's where we came in.

Absolutely everyone

Globalisation, quite as the name suggests, is the supposed 'final phase' of capitalism, nothing less than the yoking together of everyone – and that means everyone – in the same noble cause. (Those with longer memories may recall that, once upon a time, there was a supposed Communist plot to take over the entire planet, bit by bit, without anyone really noticing. Well, this is the same thing, run by different economists.)

This means wealth and comfort for those in charge, but what does it mean to the latecomers, the 'developing' nations of the globe who are being asked to sign up to the scheme? In the words of one journalist that everyone should read, Greg Palast:

> The spiky-haired protestors in the streets of Seattle believe there's some kind of grand conspiracy between the corporate powers, the IMF [International Monetary Fund] and an alphabet soup of agencies that work to suck the blood of Bolivians and steal gold from Tanzania. But the tree-huggers are wrong: the details are far more stomach-churning than even they imagine.

Palast's star witness is a good one: Joseph Stiglitz, the World Bank's former chief economist. Stiglitz provided Palast with papers showing that the IMF had knowingly provoked riots and disorder by pushing up the prices of basic commodities in Third World countries. The process of enslaving poorer nations is a four-step swindle, in which the victim nation's wide-eyed awe at the riches of the huckster plays a central role. After the World Bank and IMF have been on a fact-finding tour of the victim nation, they dangle a series of grants and aid packages and announce that the country should take a stiff dose of Step One.

1 – Privatisation. Victim countries are persuaded to flog off publicly owned utilities to kick-start their economies (it supposedly guarantees more money in circulation, better competition owing to the free market, and so on).

2 – Free up your borders. Being part of the New Global Economy means free trade with foreign nations – so abolish your laws that prevent money leaving the country. Oddly enough, it's at about this stage that money starts leaving the country.

3 – Raise prices. In order to strengthen your economy (which may be haemorrhaging money wildly, but give it time to settle), you must raise the prices of basic commodities, thus encouraging the free market to start providing cheaper alternatives. At this stage, something happens that Stiglitz calls the 'IMF Riot'. A secret World Bank document about Ecuador, for example, stated that this process would almost certainly spark 'public unrest'. Which is one way of putting it. In 1998, the abolition of food and fuel subsidies in Indonesia resulted in nationwide disturbances.

4 – Free trade. That's free trade for us, not you. The victim country now finds itself obliged to accept vast amounts of imports from 'developed' countries, while virtually unable to export anything of its own and struggling to pay off the loans it was foolishly sweet-talked into accepting.

3: Towards the hive planet

Ultimately, Stiglitz was fired from the World Bank for expressing an interest in studying why its policies ended so consistently in disaster.

Stiglitz is a key insider and his version of events has been supported by another 'defector', John Perkins, who worked for Chas T. Main, a US company contracted to carry out research for the World Bank on Third World nations, and who told his story in *Confessions of an Economic Hit Man* (2004).

> My real job was giving loans to other countries, huge loans, much bigger than they could possibly repay ... The poor people in these countries would be stuck ultimately with this amazing debt that they couldn't possibly repay. A country like Ecuador today owes over 50 per cent of its national budget just to pay down its debts. So we have them over a barrel. When we want more oil, we go to Ecuador and say: 'Look, you're not able to repay your debts, so give our oil companies your Amazon rainforests, which are full of oil.' So we make a big loan, most of it comes back to the United States, the country is left with the debt plus lots of interest and they basically become our servants, our slaves.

Perkins claims:

> Economic hit men are highly paid professionals who cheat countries around the globe out of trillions of dollars. They funnel money from the World Bank, the US Agency for International Development (USAID), and other foreign 'aid' organizations into the coffers of huge corporations and the pockets of a few wealthy families who control the planet's natural resources. Their tools include fraudulent financial reports, rigged elections, payoffs, extortion, sex, and murder. They play a game as old as empire, but one that has taken on new and terrifying dimensions during this time of globalization.

Reviewers went mad over Perkins's claims, but his first boss at Main, Einar Greve said:

> I would say that, allowing for some author discretion, basically his story is true.
>
> What John's book says is, there was a conspiracy to put all these countries on the hook, and that happened. Whether or not it was some sinister plot or not is up to interpretation, but many of these countries are still over the barrel and have never been able to repay the loans.

The US State Department denied in strong language Perkins's claim of a personal connection to America's National Security Agency, but admitted:

> *Confessions of an Economic Hit Man*, which Perkins says has been translated into some 20 languages, is popular because it is an exciting, first-person, cloak-and-dagger tale that plays to popular images about alleged US economic exploitation of Third World countries. Perkins raises legitimate questions about the impacts of economic growth and modernization on developing countries and indigenous peoples.

Ever wondered why they don't teach basic economics in school? Then you've probably never wondered why muggers don't teach karate.

'The Internet as a Tool for Preserving the Status Quo'

'The Internet has vast potential for enabling people in the developing world to engage in freer local economic and political activity, with far-reaching implications at the macroeconomic and national political levels. This is by no means a one-way street, however. Entrenched economic and political interests will be able to use the Internet as a tool for maintaining their dominant positions, especially because they typically command greater resources and coercive authority.

'The ways in which this phenomenon may be observed include the following:

- Disruption of communications through attacks on servers or virus introductions into sites considered to be undesirable
- Surreptitious interception and reading of communications; noting originators and recipients of encrypted communications
- Introduction of disinformation into newsgroups and chat rooms, including the appropriation of user identities to induce confusion or discord
- Blockage of access to sites considered to be undesirable

'Probably the most powerful, the potential to flood Internet news and information channels with material that reflects a government's position on issues.

'In addition to these means of defending entrenched interests, local economic or political entities in many developing countries would face few restraints on the use of coercive measures, such as:

- Damaging or confiscating computers
- Forcing the shutdown of web sites
- Intimidating individuals known or suspected to be using the Internet in ways that threaten established economic or political interests.'
  - From: 'E-Commerce at the Grass Roots', prepared for the National Intelligence Council, 30 June 2000

That's all, folks

University of Washington psychologist Elizabeth Loftus has implanted false memories in people, using adverts.

Loftus's department created a fake print advertisement describing a visit to Disneyland, a flier with Bugs Bunny standing in front of a Disney placard (Bugs Bunny is of course a Warner Bros character who would never be encountered there). She then selected volunteers who had been to Disneyland in earlier life, and exposed them to this advert while telling them that they were being asked to evaluate the quality of the advert's copy.

Later, 33 per cent of her subjects claimed they had met Bugs Bunny at Disneyland. The false memory rate was boosted when people were given multiple exposures to the fake advertisement. In one study, 36 per cent of those given three exposures said they met Bugs Bunny, compared to only 9 per cent in a control condition.

Loftus's collaborator Jacquie Pickrell said: 'The frightening thing about this study is that it suggests how easily a false memory can be created.'

Or did she?

3½

The End

Johann Kovacs, a railway porter at Bihar in Hungary, had yesterday a narrow escape of being dissected alive. Two days ago he fell down unconscious while at work and was taken to the hospital. The doctors pronounced him dead and a post-mortem was decided upon, for which all preparations were made, the body being put on the dissecting table, where a lecture was delivered over it to the students before the body was opened. At the first prick of the knife, Kovacs awoke with a start, and as soon as he realised his position, endeavoured to assault the surgeon who held the dissecting knife. He had to be forcibly restrained by the other doctors.
— *Daily Express*, 24 July 1907

'Old Mother' Djao, said to be the most notorious blood-thirsty bandit the province of Sianthung ever produced, has been executed at Ichowfu in Shantung, according to reports received in Shanghai by mission organisations, says Reuter. 'The unfortunate woman underwent that most fearsome of Chinese death penalties, the ling-che, or in English, the slicing process ... 'Ling-che is vivisection, done by experts in such a manner that the victim survives in a conscious state through hours of a terrible ordeal.'
— *Morning Post*, (n.d.) 1924

Where is thy sting? Oh ...

Thinking of becoming an organ donor when you die? In order for you to donate major organs, such as kidneys, heart or lungs, they have to be fresh. That means they have to be full of oxygen-rich blood. That means the donor's heart has to be beating (pumping the vital fluid round the body) until the moment the organs are cut out.

There is no legal requirement to give posthumous donors any anaesthetic. The reason being that prior to becoming what's known as a 'heartbeating donor' (or a 'beating-heart cadaver' in the States), you have to be declared brain-dead. In other words, you don't need drugs because you can't feel pain. (Oddly, there are no records of beating-heart organ donors turning up later to complain that they *could* in fact feel pain.)

How is brain death established? Let us assume (as we should) that you are not breathing, or are unable to breathe unaided. The basic test is loss of brainstem function (your brainstem is the bit that looks like blue broccoli at the top of your spine, underneath the big grey cauliflower of your proper brain).

Here are the essential tests medics conduct to establish brain-stem death:

(a) absence of pupillary reflex response to light
(b) absence of corneal reflexes
(c) absence of vestibulo-ocular reflex
(d) absence of cranial nerve response to pain
(e) absence of gag and cough reflexes

In plain English, someone (a) shines a light in your eye, then (b) pokes you in the eye with a cotton bud; then they (c) squirt a pipette full of cold water into your ear, (d) poke you in the side of the head and finally (e) stick a cotton bud down your throat. If you don't react to any of that, you're probably dead.

But ... but ... surely that doesn't prove that your brain is actually not working at all? You could be in there, totally unable to respond (especially if your functions are being suppressed by, say, nerve damage or poisoning by drugs).

There is a back-up system: the electro-encephalogram (EEG). This measures electrical activity taking place near the brain's surface, which is displayed as a wiggly jagged line tracing across a screen. No wiggly line, no activity.

But according to a 2003 survey of British and Irish medics, only 13 per cent of neuroanaesthetists believed that EEG 'silence' was required to back up the diagnosis of brainstem death. (Bafflingly, 75 per cent of the same group claimed that they would give anaesthetic to a brainstem-dead organ donor: why they claim to waste valuable drugs on people they sincerely believe to be dead is in no way explained.)

So, how dead is dead? In the words of one medical paper:

> A patient with brainstem infarction met the clinical criteria for brain death but had persistent EEG activity, complicating our decision to withdraw life support. ... [Blood flow information] led us to withdraw life support, despite the presence of EEG activity.

Still doubting this?

Ask consultant anaesthetist Philip Keep of Norfolk and Norwich Hospital, who in 2000 confided to millions of BBC radio listeners that he refused to carry a donor card because there is no legal obligation to provide anaesthetics to 'dead' patients. His comments were provoked by an editorial in *Anaesthesia*, the journal of the Royal College of Anaesthetists, which deplored the lack of legislation demanding routine anaesthesia in operations to remove organs from brainstem-dead patients.

'I will not carry a donor card for that very reason,' he said.

Discussing his comments, *The Times* (20 August 2000) noted that: 'Many experts argue that the twitches of a donor on the operating table are just reflexive actions.'

You want fries with that?

Are you out of your mind?

Despite the posturings of the high priests of science and spirituality, no one knows where consciousness comes from, or where it is at any given moment, or where it goes at death (if it goes anywhere at all, either way).

The spiritually inclined claim that out-of-body and near-death experiences show that the 'mind' exists independently of the body (dualism).

The scientifically inclined claim that the surgical alteration of personality shows that the mind is a product of the body (epiphenomenalism).

Neither camp knows the truth, and so you shouldn't get suckered into believing either one.

Obviously, the scientists seem more persuasive at first glance: but their explanations are more than a little reliant on wishful thinking about things they don't understand yet, like Columbus scanning the horizon and hoping his crew hasn't run out of rum.

One classic example of this is the 'consciousness as an emergent quantum property' gambit, very popular in recent years.

You only need to understand three things to comprehend this theory:

1. Quantum physics deals with entities so unimaginably strange and tiny that they don't even exist except as

energy levels and are next door to impossible to understand.

2. 'Emergent' means that if you take something and keep adding more of it to itself, 'more' becomes 'different' (think of a single ant and a nest full).

3. There is not the slightest shred of evidence for any of the theory.

Another way of thinking about consciousness among really hard-core scientists is to simply dismiss consciousness as 'an illusion'.

No one has yet tried to explain what it is, exactly, that might be experiencing this alleged 'illusion'. This is not to say that the dualists (including the major religions of the world) do not have some serious problems, too, because they do. So much so that we'll not embarrass them by talking about it.

Anyway, there is no final answer as yet.

And when there is, probably both sides will have been wrong on some of it.

Mind you, you really do have to admire a phenomenon capable of arguing in favour of its own non-existence.

What IS that out there?

Since the Enlightenment (roughly, the bit between the Renaissance and the Industrial Revolution), it has been generally agreed by the scientific community that what we perceive is actually an illusion of sorts.

This book might look as if it has a coloured cover and slightly off-white pages, but it doesn't really.
What you're looking at is actually your brain's creation, a sort of 'artist's impression' that you use to make sense of the world

around you. Inside your head, this information is woven together into a coherent whole. Outside your head, it's a sort of dark chaos. Your senses – a stream of electricity along conductive fibres – cobble together a few wavelengths of electromagnetic radiation into colours and shapes, a few vibrations into sounds and a few chemical reactions into tastes and smells. Everything you experience is simply the result of neurons in your brain firing in different patterns. There's no 'there' out there.

But what if – just suppose, for the sake of argument – the world really did look like that? What if this book really was exactly the way it seems? What if the colours are actually real, and the pages really do have the texture you perceive them to have? What if, instead of being a framed and colourless square with certain frequencies of radiation streaming through it, the window in your wall was actually white round the edges, transparent in the middle, and the tree you could see through it really was brown and green? That the birdsong actually sounded the way you think it does? No, sorry, perhaps that's too ridiculous. Forget I mentioned it.

Remember this, though. No matter how many times your neurons fire in a certain way when you look up at the blueness of the sky, you do not experience your neurons firing. What you experience is the colour blue.

At some point – if the Enlightenment view of perception is to be believed – your brain converts the firing of neurons into the artificial perception of 'blueness'. The process by which this happens is no nearer explanation now than it ever was. But perhaps there's another explanation. Perhaps the sky really is blue.

'I chose the path towards light'

Ten per cent of resuscitated hospital patients are believed to have conscious memories of events after their deaths.

Patients who had been declared brain dead could recall conversations between the medical staff trying to revive them. Other flatliners reported out-of-body experiences in which they observed people and objects that they couldn't have seen from their position, even if their heart, breathing and brain activity hadn't been absent at the time in question.

Sam Parnia, clinical research fellow in pulmonary and internal medicine at Southampton University, studied sixty-three resuscitated heart-attack patients, seven of whom described classic near-death experiences. Retired British Airways employee Patrick Tierney told him:

> There was a long dim corridor branching into light or darkness.

> I chose the path towards light and found myself in this area of fantastic bright colour, which could have been a garden.

Dr Parnia said:

> These patients should not have been capable of thought because they had no brain function. In fact, there has never been any proof that the brain generates thoughts. We believe many doctors have witnessed this phenomenon but have not discussed it for fear of being laughed at.

Needless to say, Dr Parnia got laughed at.

Out of sight, out of mind

The near-death experience – you know, the whole business with the tunnel of light, the brilliant pure light at the end and the mysterious voice saying 'gooo baaack' – has now been explained. The tunnel of light is actually the random firing of neurons as the brain shuts down. It has been proven, you see, that the 'white noise' effect that this creates produces a hallucinatory sensation of spinning (you can get something of the same effect by staring at the static on an untuned TV screen). The pure white light at the end of the tunnel? It's actually the gradual failure of the nervous system, producing a blind spot in your vision that your brain interprets as being blindingly white. Because this blind spot grows and gets bigger, the dying person gets the illusion of travelling along a tunnel towards a pure white light.

In other words, this is all an illusion caused by the chaotic disintegration of the brain's networks. By the time you reach the bright white light, the chaos is at its maximum. You are dead. (Never mind the transplant team waiting by the bedside, assuming they haven't started on you already.)

Where does that leave near-death experiencers who pass into the light? They come back reporting coherent and similar experiences – loved ones standing near, a presence of pure benevolence, a sort of natural and rural setting. Moreover, there is a historical tendency for widely separated brains, in different epochs and cultures, to produce very similar hallucinations at the point of death.

This just goes to show that biologically, we're all the same deep down. In other words, at the point of its greatest confusion and maximum disintegration, your brain suddenly produces a stable and coherent hallucination – and it's pretty much the same whoever you are.
Anyone who has ever thrown a handful of china fragments at the floor in order to make themselves a new plate will be able to understand this plain truth.

NFB

GP medical note code for: 'Not For Burning.' British GPs collect a £34 fee for simply filling in a cremation form, known in the trade as 'ash cash'.

Notes

1: YOU AND YOURS

Where did all the Neanderthals go?: There have been five great extinctions in the history of life on earth. We are officially living through the sixth. For an introduction see
<http://rewilding.org/thesixthgreatextinction.htm>

The reason for the disappearance of the Neanderthals is often described as 'unknown' in the history books. Presumably, it is only the convenient absence of modern-day Neanderthal lawyers that prevents charges of 'Neanderthal holocaust denial' from being brought. We killed them. And we may even have eaten them. Just like we killed and/or ate everything else. We're hard-wired for genocide. That's how evolution works and that's why you're reading this rather than picking fleas off your arse while seated up a tree.

Discourse on Method: Don't let anyone tell you otherwise. There's no more a scientific method than there's a 'learning-to-ride-a-bike' method. You just keep doing it until you get it right.

Why is Mboy Dcik so hard to read?: The stupid email quoted at the head of this piece has been doing the rounds for a year or two now, and never fails to trick people into believing it. Possibly even the person who wrote it actually believed it. Real-life 'researchers' at Cambridge University have no idea where it came from – see
<www.snopes.com/language/apocryph/cambridge.asp>
To cite John Gatto – whose great work on this subject I can only reflect in this section:

> According to the *Journal of the American Medical Association* (December 1995), 33 percent of all patients cannot read and understand instructions on how often to take medication, notices about doctor's appointments, consent forms, labels on prescription bottles, insurance forms, and other simple parts of self-care. They are rendered helpless by inability to read. Concerning those behind the nation's prison walls (a population that has tripled since 1980), the National Center for Education

Statistics stated in a 1996 report that 80 percent of all prisoners could not interpret a bus schedule, understand a news article or warranty instructions, or read maps, schedules, or payroll forms. Nor could they balance a checkbook. Forty percent could not calculate the cost of a purchase
— *The Underground History of American Education*

La, la, la, not listening: Charles Fort recognised this phenomenon nearly a century ago. In Chapter XVII of *The Book of the Damned*, he mentioned our genuine tendency to forget uncomfortable facts as follows:

But the dimness of the datum of only two chapters ago. The carved stone disk of Tarbes, and the rain that fell every afternoon for twenty – if I haven't forgotten, myself, whether it was twenty-three or twenty-five days! – upon one small area. We are all Thomsons, with brains that have smooth and slippery, though corrugated, surfaces – or that all intellection is associative – or that we remember that which correlates with a dominant – and a few chapters go by, and there's scarcely an impression that hasn't slid off our smooth and slippery brains, of Leverrier and the 'planet Vulcan.'

There are two ways by which irreconcilables can be remembered – if they can be correlated in a system more nearly real than the system that rejects them – and by repetition and repetition and repetition.

Did I say that out loud?: This is *the* classic faux-pas on the hidden social engineering agenda of modern US schooling: 'You're not going to be taught much, because you're never going to need it. We'll keep the Latin and piano lessons, you get the most basic literacy and how to obey orders.' If this gave you a start, you'll probably enjoy John Taylor Gatto's *Underground History of American Education* (see **Furthering Reading**).

Go to the top of the class: Does anyone actually doubt this?

Did you feel sorry for the fat kid?: *The Guardian*, 12 December 1996.

A problem shared is a problem spread: Kruger and Dunning's original paper can be read at
<www.apa.org/journals/features/psp7761121.pdf>

Think of the number of times that you've done something that you were later told should have been beyond you. Don't listen when people tell you you can't do things – it's the modern-day equivalent of a curse. Use your innate ability to ignore unpleasant information (see 'La, la, la ...' above).

Kid versus whizz-kid: *The Daily Telegraph*, 14 March 2002.

Strangely, although you often hear of infant prodigies in the mathematical and musical fields, Tia Roberts's remarkable coup doesn't seem to have attracted any of the attention it might appear to warrant. Could it be that the 'whizz-kids' of the banks are just either lucky or unlucky? That the bear pit is merely a pinstriped version of the bookie? That it's the sheer amount of money in motion at any one moment that prevents the whole thing going 'pop'?

Sweet sixteen, never been ... nah ...: Early puberty: *The Observer*, 18 June 2000; early contraception: *The Daily Telegraph*, 3 February 1999.

This is an uncomfortable one to talk about in today's climate of panic about paedophilia. But can anyone deny that children today seem to be maturing earlier? The current wave of underage offenders might just be bored adults trapped in children's bodies.

Stranger than friction: Chinn's research: *The Times*, 18 March 2000.

Fear of strangers: *The Guardian*, 4 August 1999.

767,000 and £1,400,000,000 p/a: *The Guardian*, 21 July 1999 and 13 July 2004; *The Times*, 1 August 1998.

Well, don't just sit there. The Advisory Service for Squatters publish *The Squatter's Handbook* and can be contacted on 020 3216 0099.

£230,000,000:
<www.guardian.co.uk/crime/article/0,,1741043,00.html>
£26,527,108,436,994:
<www.publications.parliament.uk/pa/cm200506/cmselect/cmpubacc/1079/1079.pdf>

Chuck your passport: This really can be done. Although you'll need a bit of money, or luck, and ideally both. For further advice on starting your own country – or on joining one of the many 'micronations' now on offer to the discerning citizen of the world – visit: <www.micronations.net>. Take careful note, however, of the number of optimistic micronations that have ended up being used as fronts for money-laundering or drug-smuggling.

God save the Queen (from detection): The graves of George and Hannah's offspring: *The Times*, 31 December 2000; also Michael Thornton: *Royal Feud*, 1985.

2,000: *The Daily Telegraph*, 5 March 2000.

£1,200 and **£3,000,000:** *The Observer*, 6 December 1998.

An apple a day:
<http://bmj.bmjjournals.com/cgi/content/full/320/7249/1561>

This effect is emphatically not caused by doctors failing to sign death certificates while striking. The truth of this is shown by the fact that there is no corresponding 'spike' in backlogged deaths being registered *after* a doctors' strike finishes.

225,000 deaths by medic: See Dr Barbara Starfield of Johns Hopkins School of Hygiene and Public Health, *Journal of the American Medical Association*, July 2000. Various versions of (and commentaries on) her text are available online. Take your pick.

One reason for what is called *iatrogenesis* (illnesses created by healers) is the decidedly interventionist nature of modern western medicine. A book you may care to investigate is Robert Mendelson's *Confessions of a Medical Heretic* – still in print after nearly thirty years. In this, Mendelson poses a mock medical test: 'Your patient has a pimple on his nose.' The options are (a) give him some ointment and tell him to come back if the spot isn't gone within a week; or (b) rush him to intensive care, pump him full of every antibiotic on the market, stick him on a heart-lung machine to keep him functioning and cut his head off to avoid the disease spreading. Mendelson says that students who answer along the lines of answer (b) are more likely to pass their exams. He then spends a good deal of time proving to the satisfaction of readers that although his mock test is an exaggeration, it's not an altogether unrealistic one.

Possible Lemsip side-effects: in-packet leaflet.

Made-up drugs: *The Guardian*, 24 June 1998.

Nothing works better than Aspirin (so take nothing): Park L and Covi L: 'Non-blind placebo trial', *Archives of General Psychiatry*, 1965,

Vol. 12, pp336–45, available online at
<www.anxiousmind.com/images/placebo-trial.pdf>

The ring of confidence (tricks): For much more than you want to know, see Christopher Bryson's *The Fluoride Deception* (Seven Stories Press, 2004). But be careful who you talk to about it – suspicion about fluoridation has been the hallmark of the crank for years. It won't help to point out that this popular perception of crankiness is the deliberate side-effect of an audacious pro-fluoride propaganda campaign masterminded by Edward Bernays in the 1960s, either – even though it's perfectly true, it'll just make you seem even more paranoid.

Purrranoia:
<www.guardian.co.uk/science/story/0,,1920165,00.html> or see Peter Cushing in *The Uncanny.*

Sssssssssssshhhh: This one won't earn you any friends. But it happens to be true.
Smoking and diet.
<http://news.bbc.co.uk/1/hi/health/1309091.stm>

Apple-eating: *The Times*, 20 January 2000

Dr Kenneth Denson: *The Times* 22 November 1999

For the Tom and Jerry ruling, see:
<http://www.ofcom.org.uk/tv/obb/prog_cb/obb67/issue67.pdf>
Further information about animation that's sliding down an Orwellian memory hole can be examined in great detail at
<http://looney.goldenagecartoons.com/ltcuts/>

Patients often recognised normality when staff did not: Rosenhan's justly notorious experiment can be read about in detail at
<http://www.stanford.edu/~kocabas/onbeingsane.pdf>
Gert Postel: *The Times*, 21 January 2001.

Give a dog: Poor old Wayne and his criminal record: *The Times*, 5 July 2000.

Bzzzt: *The Observer,* 8 December 1996.

Why do doctors have such bad handwriting?: *Health Service Journal*, 19 December 1997.

A spoonful of sugar: See **Furthering Reading**.

This won't hurt: *The Guardian*, 6 April 1998.

Bzzzzzzzzzzzzzzzzzzzzt!: The Milgram experiment can be read about in depth at the Milgram website <www.stanleymilgram.com/milgram.php>
Milgram's reflections on his achievement can be read at <http://home.swbell.net/revscat/perilsOfObedience.html>

My office - now: Robert Hare's remarks: *Daily Express,* 31 August 2002.

Snakes in Suits: When Psychopaths go to Work (Barnes and Noble)

2: POLITICS BY OTHER MEANS

Progress: Dying to escape: *The Guardian*, 30 October 1998; regional suicide rates: *The Guardian*, 9 September 1998

Adman of mass destruction: See **Furthering Reading**. Also see, if you can get hold of it, Adam Curtis's 2002 BBC documentary series on the Freud dynasty, *Century of the Self*. Come to that, see anything Curtis has ever made, especially *Pandora's Box* and *The Living Dead*.

How DO they get away with it? The Pitts: *The Guardian*, 6 October 1998. John Major's Trafalgar: *The Express*, 15 October 2005.
Israeli poll: *The Guardian* 15 December 2001.

Americans and those missing WMD: <www.worldpublicopinion.org/pipa/articles/brunitedstatescanadara/238.php?nid=&id=&pnt=238&lb=brusc>

Geocentric Americans: <www.nytimes.com/2005/08/30/science/30profile.html?ei=5070&en631977063>

Egyptian poll: <www.dailystaregypt.com/article.aspx?ArticleID=3404>
Clinton's upstanding defence: *The Independent*, 16 January 1999.

'His lips moved': See **Furthering Reading**.

Don't watch my hands (#1): Full text of the Blair memo:
<www.news.bbc.co.uk/1/hi/uk_politics/836822.stm>
'It is bizarre that any government I lead...': Is it really so bizarre that a Blair-led government could be open to such charges? Tony Blair and his wife, Cherie Booth, have each gone on the record with comments about their sex life, printed in the British tabloid press (namely, the *S*n*). What effect this might have upon the psyches of the couple's children can only be imagined. Prior to this, son Euan was found

unconscious in his own vomit in Leicester Square, London, hours after his father had announced yet another of his pipe dreams (that is, 'initiatives'). This one – curiously enough – was about punishing the disorderly by marching them to the nearest ATM to pay instant fines. In 2004, daughter Kathryn

'The Martin case...': Refers to British farmer Tony Martin, who in 2000 fatally shot a young man who had broken into his farmhouse. Martin – who had taken to keeping a shotgun by his bedside after a string of burglaries in which the police had failed to capture the culprits – received a hefty prison sentence. The Martin case created an unplanned media debate. Public sentiment, which had been whipped up into a seething state over preceding years by the Blair government's 'law and order' agenda, unexpectedly came down on Martin's side. The same prime minister who found time to call for the 'release' of Coronation Street character Deirdre Barlow (who was 'wrongfully imprisoned' for the fictional murder of her equally non-existent husband) was apparently struck dumb throughout.

Babies of mass destruction: Stick it in Google if you don't believe me.

Grow your own terrorists: NATO's Secret Armies: See the excellent *Operation Gladio and Terrorism in Western Europe* by Daniele Ganser (Frank Cass Ltd, 2005). One of the biggest questions in the Gladio story is the extent to which Britain's Gladio cells might have played a role in the manoeuvrings against Prime Minister Harold Wilson, who was the subject of at least two separate attempts at mounting a military coup (in 1968 and 1975). The Ramsay/Dorrill *Smear! Wilson and the Secret State* is your next port of call for that, though ...

Woodsmen of mass destruction: The National Security Archive's version of *The Operation Northwoods Papers* can be read here: <www.gwu.edu/~nsarchiv/news/20010430>

Obviously, there are uncomfortably uncanny resonances with some of the conspiracy theories about 9/11 (right down to the remote-controlled planes and fake funerals). Not to worry, though: The US State Department has produced a guide to 'Identifying

Misinformation', which should help sort you out:
<http://usinfo.state.gov/media/misinformation.html>

As one contributor to *Lobster* magazine observed: 'It certainly puts paid to the theory that Americans have no sense of irony.'

Back, and to the ... right: See at Robin Ramsay in **Furthering Reading**. You may also like to stick <LBJ, wink> into a search engine's 'images' option. The other man in the photo is – well, suffice to say that it will take you ten minutes to find out, but hardly a single JFK researcher on the conspiracy or nonspiracy side knows who he is. Or what the deeper meaning might be behind his wink...

Or you can just take the word of the lazy, jaded dullards who scoff at any mention of conspiracies in any context whatsoever and who, when JFK is mentioned, will usually make 'jokes' about Lord Lucan riding Shergar.

The latter route is the easiest, to be honest.

Gentlemen prefer greys: Yes, I thought you'd want to check this one. This CIA document appeared during a massive FOIA release in the 1990s and for a few years hung about in limbo as it seemed too fantastical to be true. This wouldn't be the first time a forged CIA document has appeared in the National Archives.

One very famous example of this is the memo 'proving' that JFK's alleged assassin was a CIA agent. You can see the memo here:
<http://www.prisonplanet.com/articles/september2004/160904oswaldwascia.htm>

and read an explanation of why it's a fake here:
<http://mccone-rowley.blogspot.com/2005/09/larry-hancock-on-mccone-rowley-from.html>

But the Monroe 'things from outer space' wiretap was later inadvertently authenticated *by the CIA itself*, and you can read about this peculiar little story here: <http://www.blackmesapress.com/page4.htm>

(Disclaimer: besides the backstory to the memo, the site's editors go on to use the memo as evidence indicating part of a grand UFO cover-up conspiracy. That's their opinion and they're welcome to it.)

'Bases in Cuba...': This remains mysterious, but may refer to the Cuban Missile crisis – or even to US military bases such as 'Camp X-Ray' (better known to the world as Guantánamo Bay).

'Kill Fidel Castro...': It is still fashionable in some left-wing circles to maintain that prior to his assassination on 22 November 1963, JFK was seeking a dialogue with Cuba's communist leader, Fidel Castro. Perhaps this is because (despite being populated by hardened Cold Warriors from top to bottom) the Kennedy White House was so good at presenting an early love-and-peace 'flower power' public relations image. In the words of *Lobster* editor Robin Ramsay: 'This argument should now cease ... The Kennedys were planning a coup which would result in Castro's death.' (*Lobster* 51, Summer 2006). Having rejected Operation Northwoods [*qv*], the Kennedys had an invasion of Cuba planned for just nine days after the day JFK got his head blown off. See: <wbostonreview.net/BR28.5/galbraith.html>

On yet another hand, Kennedy had made a speech to the UN on 20 September 1963, proposing a joint USA/USSR moon landing. In National Security Action Memorandum (NSAM) 271, addressed to NASA, Kennedy demanded a 'program of substantive co-operation with the Soviet Union in the field of outer space ... including co-operation in lunar landing programs'.

He went on to state: 'I would like an interim report on the progress of our planning by December 15.' See *Lobster* 48 and:
<www.birmo.co.uk/jfk/work_in_progress/index.htm>

Forget all the crap 'tinfoil hat'-type jokes: The question seriously has to be asked: Is there anyone in power in the USA who *didn't* have a motive for assassinating JFK?

One of Milgram's 35 per cent:
<www.armscontrol.ru/start/publications/petrov.htm>
Read more about twenty accidents that nearly caused the end of the human race: <www.nuclearfiles.org/menu/key-issues/nuclear-weapons/issues/accidents/20-mishaps-maybe-caused-nuclear-war.htm>

Don't watch my hands (#2):
Luntz memo: <www.ewg.org:16080/briefings/luntzmemo/>
A 'focus group', in case you were wondering, is a device employed by PR agents to discover what 'the people at the grassroots are really thinking'. Typically, this means seven middle-aged white people talking about newspapers with an opinion pollster, while sipping warm white wine and eating cheap snacks in a hotel conference room.

Unspeak by Steven Poole (Little, Brown, 2006): Don't be misled by the light-hearted tone of the quotes in *Mind Bombs*. *Unspeak* is a dark and complex book that encompasses subjects from anti-social behaviour orders (Asbos) to the redefinition of the word 'torture'.

Weather of mass destruction: See Kathleen Hall-Jamieson's book in **Furthering Reading**.

Waterway of mass destruction: The first proper overview of the attempts to nobble Nasser appeared in *The Guardian*, 20 August 1998, previewing Stephen Dorril's then-forthcoming book *MI6: Fifty Years of Special Operations* (Fourth Estate, 2000). The relevant pages in Dorril are 613-33 and 639. Details can also be found in Peter Wright's *Spycatcher* (Viking Penguin, 1987) on pp160-3.

Weapons of we are not amused destruction: *Fenian Fire: The British Government Plot to Assassinate Queen Victoria* by Christy Campbell (Harper Collins, 2002)

Hattersley's review of *Fenian Fire*:
<http://observer.guardian.co.uk/review/story/0,6903,722150,00.html>

£990,000,000: *The Guardian*, quoting Saferworld, 03 July 2001

£6,000,000,000: *The Guardian* 10 November 2004

The which Blair project: Dr Allan Beveridge:
<http://politics.guardian.co.uk/labour/story/0,9061,1096763,00.html>
The Political Animal by Jeremy Paxman (Penguin, 2002)
Tony Blair: The Man Who Lost His Smile by Leo Abse (Robson Books, 2003)
The 'handicapped smile': <www.valeriesinason.com/
sinason%20contribution%20to%20psychotherapy.htm>
Matthew Parris/'Blair delusional':
<www.timesonline.co.uk/article/0,,1065-2091566,00.html>
An excellent pocket analysis of Blair's upside-down logic:
<http://comment.independent.co.uk/commentators/article2081570.ece>

The things they say (#1): <http://politics.guardian.co.uk/iraq/
comment/0,12956,1036687,00.html>

Oh, say can you see?: That missing flag:
<www.editorandpublisher.com/eandp/news/
article_display.jsp?vnu_content_id=1003052001>
David Friend's *Watching the World Change*:

<http://www.holtzbrinckpublishers.com/FSG/search/
SearchBookDisplay.asp?BookKey=3462073>

Don't watch my hands (#3): Two examples to get you started:
Tony Blair leaving Downing Street right after being interviewed by
police over 'cash for peerages' allegations (15 December 2006):
<http://politics.guardian.co.uk/funding/story/0,,1973100,00.html>
– right side – confident; left side – 'oh shiiit'.

George W. Bush caught mid-improvisation at a White House press conference (as featured on the front of *Private Eye*, November 2006):
<http://www.ugandandiscussions.co.uk/1171/>
– right side – folksy, upbeat; left side – 'er ... prompt?'

The things they say (#2):
Bush and Blair, 31 January 2003:
<www.whitehouse.gov/news/releases/2003/01/20030131-23.html>
Clark, 15 June 2003: Oddly the transcript for this one has disappeared.
But a record is preserved at: <www.fair.org/index.php?page=1842>
Cheney, 14 September 2003: Transcript at:
<www.msnbc.msn.com/id/3080244/>
Bush, 25 September 2005:
<www.whitehouse.gov/news/releases/2002/09/20020925-1.html>
Bush, 7 October 2005:
<www.whitehouse.gov/news/releases/2002/10/20021007-8.html>

Chuck your passport (#2): The Diego Garcia depopulation conspiracy
is one of several British plots discussed in *Ministries of Deception:
Cover-ups in Whitehall:* (Tim Slessor, Aurum Press, 2002)

3: Towards the hive planet

Computers vote Bush: David Dill's lecture: *The Independent*, 16
February 2004
Morris's remarks: <www.thehill.com/morris/110404.aspx>

'I've Been Murdered': See Edwin Black's book in **Furthering Reading**

Dang An: 'A black mark...':
<www.asianresearch.org/articles/2573.html>
Comments from Jian Shuo Wang (posted 16 February 2006, 01:26):
<http://home.wangjianshuo.com/archives/
20060215_20_years_of_professional_managers_in_china.htm

Interestingly, in 2004 when one IT expert went as a speaker to a Japanese conference, where he intended to make comments about the vulnerability of Japan's juki net system, he met with official resistance so stiff that he tried to sue the Japanese Government for censoring him: <www.networkworld.com/news/2004/1122ussecur.html>

34,310: <http://news.scotsman.com/topics.cfm?tid=428&id=653762006>

250,000: *The Independent on Sunday*, 20 February 2000 (not archived online).

'Hundreds of thousands':
<http://news.independent.co.uk/uk/politics/article447792.ece>
There's no indication in *The Independent*'s report of who the 'organised criminals' might be. Could it therefore be more than coincidence that shortly after this report appeared, the *Sunday Times* found that: 'The stolen identities of Britons – including their credit card details, home addresses and security passwords – are being sold on Russian websites for as little as £1 each'?
<www.timesonline.co.uk/article/0,,2087-2340900,00.html>

Hmmm. Identities being stolen from government departments and sold to Russian criminals at precisely the same time that the government was trying to promote Identity Cards ... No, forget I even mentioned it.

1,000,000: They did better than they expected, though: 'At the time of the census officials believed they could have missed 3 to 4 per cent of the population ...'
<http://www.guardian.co.uk/uk_news/story/0,3604,797185,00.html>

'Everyone': <www.telegraph.co.uk/news/main.jhtml?xml=/news/2006/10/24/ndna24.xml>

'A generation': You can read the leaked emails in full, here:
<http://www.timesonline.co.uk/article/0,,2087-2261631,00.html>

'Britain will become...': Alan Hart, ex-*Panorama*, comments on Sir Edward's remarks: 'Today I find myself wondering if that was pure speculation, or inside knowledge about how "the system's" controllers really think.' Letter to *The Guardian*, 8 November 2006.
See: <http://www.guardian.co.uk/letters/story/0,,1941916,00.html>

The one-way street of surveillance ...: Shredded files to avoid FOIA:
<http://news.independent.co.uk/uk/politics/article26029.ece>

'Asbestos contamination' [cough] at the MoD:
<http://politics.guardian.co.uk/foi/story/0,,1674302,00.html>
For explanations of each *FOIA exemption*, please see
<www.dca.gov.uk/foi/guidance/exguide/index.htm>

Lord Butler's Report can be read at

'The most spied-upon nation in the world...':
</www.timesonline.co.uk/newspaper/0,,176-2426874,00.html>
Lie detectors for benefit claimants:
<http://comment.independent.co.uk/leading_articles/
article26327.ece>
The Commissioner's views on ID cards and the National Identity Register:
<www.ico.gov.uk/upload/documents/library/corporate/detailed_
specialist_guides/id_cards_bill_-_ico_concerns_october_2005.pdf>

Prints of darkness:
Mayfield and fingerprint practice: *New Scientist*, 19 September 2005
<http://www.newscientist.com/article.ns?id=mg18725174.500>
Dror and Peron's paper – 'When Emotions Get the Better of Us: The
Effect of Contextual Top-down Processing on Matching Fingerprints' –
can be read online at <http://www.ecs.soton.ac.uk/
~id/ACP%20emotions%20&%20fingerprint%20ident.pdf>

Frozen putty fingers: Want to try this?
<www.puttyworld.com/thinputdeffi.html> is the place for you.
Woodglue and transparency method:
<www.ccc.de/biomettrie/fingerabdruck_kopieren.xml?language=en>
Matsumoto's paper, somewhat quaintly rendered into English but perfect-
ly usable, is preserved online at: <http://cryptome.org/gummy.htm>

100,000: <http://preview.tinyurl.com/v85gk>

425,033 and **600,000:**
<www.guardian.co.uk/frontpage/story/0,16518,1678168,00.html>
See also: <www.statistics.gov.uk/cci/nugget.asp?id=273>

750,000 and **3,500,000:** <www.privacyinternational.org/
article.shtml?cmd%5B347%5D=x-347-508146>

4,500,000: <http://news.bbc.co.uk/1/hi/uk/4579366.stm>

'Everyone': <www.telegraph.co.uk/news/main.jhtml?xml=/news/2006/10/24/ndna24.xml>

311 and **10,443:** <www.homeoffice.gov.uk/science-research/using-science/dna-database/?version=1>

1: 37,000,000: The Amazing Teleporting Mr Easton:
<www.theherald.co.uk/features/61131.html>
Professor Moenssens maintains the site <www.forensic-evidence.com>
The way the odds work out plus the *Arizona example*:
<www.maa.org/devlin/devlin_10_06.html>

Absolutely everyone: Einar Greve on Perkins:
<www.tucsoncitizen.com/news/local/011705a1_tsunamiaid/1>
US State Department quasi-denial:
<http://usinfo.state.gov/media/Archive/2006/Feb/02-767147.html>

'The Internet as a Tool for Preserving the Status Quo':
<www.fas.org/irp/nic/grass_roots.htm>
The Federation of American Scientists, whose website this is, was originally formed from the (perhaps guilt-stricken) veterans of the USA's Manhattan Project, who decided that scientists had a moral obligation to keep citizens informed about weighty matters of state. Today, their project has become a multi-thousand-page open archive, stuffed full of leaked documents and other information. If you're interested in finding out about the way the intelligence communities operate, this resource should be one of your bookmarked favourites.

That's all, folks:
<http://today.uci.edu/news/release_detail.asp?key=974>
www.sciencedaily.com/releases/2001/06/010612065657.htm

3½: The End

Where is thy sting? Oh ...: Absence of reflexes test-list:
<www.medindia.net/articles/article3.asp#dia>
Neuroanaesthetists and EEG 'silence':
<http://bja.oxfordjournals.org/cgi/content/full/92/5/633>
'A patient with brainstem infarction...':
<www.ncbi.nlm.nih.gov/entrez/query.fcgi?cmd=Retrieve&db=PubMed&list_uids=3494570&dopt=Abstract>

Furthering Reading

This isn't a textbook, so there's no bibliography and no 'set texts' – you're a grown-up and quite capable of deciding what to read about. But then again, it's always hard knowing where to start. Let's assume total wide-eyed innocence in you, and you can skim over the following until you find something that catches your eyes. Perhaps you will find this list banal. Go and read something else, then.

The following are some recommended resources that you might enjoy if you've enjoyed this one – or even if it's just mildly interested you. Some of these you'll have heard of, some of them you won't. Most of the books are still in print and easily available, and anyway, there is no excuse for not being able to track them down through the excellent second-hand book-search facilities on the modern miracle of the Internet. (Just make sure you use a net café to browse for them or your search history might ring alarm bells at the local council offices – don't put any idiocy or paranoia beyond the stalker state.)

None of these is difficult, obscure, thrown in for snob value or otherwise intended as a waste of time. Each and every one will throw up more leads for you to pursue at your pleasure – and you can find your own way after that.

In no particular order, then:

Never ignore periodicals and newspapers. This is where new stuff is being pushed under your nose every day of every week. The bulk of the information you are looking for is here, even though you'd never know it to look at page one.

General circulation newspapers include *The Guardian* (www.guardian.co.uk), the only British newspaper owned by a not-for-profit corporation. Painfully right-on at times, but generally an enlightened read that will surprise you at least once a week.

The Independent (www.independent.com) is the next best British newspaper by a very small and tightening margin. *The Times* and *Daily Telegraph* (and their Sunday incarnations) complete the set.

The Lancet and the **British Medical Journal** are both what you might call 'establishment' medical journals, but they cover some of the most interesting developments in medical thought and are not averse to reporting work by the occasional heretic. Don't bother with **Nature**, which is possibly the most reactionary scientific publication in existence today and certainly the only one in the last two decades to print a suggestion that a book be burned. Shame on them.

On the other hand, the quintessentially English journal **Fortean Times** is the best place to keep track of developments (and non-starters) on the radical fringes of science and philosophy. Very much a product of the stoned and unreformed 1970s, it can always be guaranteed to raise a smile when it isn't raising a frown. Further details from <www.forteantimes.com>

New Scientist (<www.newscentist.com>) should be on everyone's sub-scription wish list – a well-designed, well-written and fairly open-minded mainstream science magazine that can be enjoyed by laymen and specialists alike.

For tittle-tattle about those in high places (not to mention the occasional bit of heavyweight journalism), **Private Eye** is a fortnightly little magazine that really ought to have folded years ago, but staggers from libel case to libel case thanks to the donations of its devoted readers.

A realistic count of high-quality, down-to-earth and reliable 'conspiracy' magazines would bring you to a total of one. **Lobster: The Journal of Parapolitics** is a twice-yearly magazine that examines all areas of political chicanery with articles, historical notes and pages of book reviews. Written 'from the hip' by a number of contributors including editor Robin Ramsay, it's available in print for £3 an issue, or via <www.lobster-magazine.co.uk>

Any book by Mr Ramsay is worth tracking down, but his legendary 1991 col-laboration with Stephen Dorrill: **Smear! Wilson and the Secret State** (Fourth Estate) will tell you more about the nature of the forces at work behind the scenes in Britain than it is possible to feel comfortable knowing. By contrast, Ramsay's compact yet comprehensive **Who Shot JFK?** (Pocket Essentials, 2002) will be a breath of fresh air to anyone who has bruised their brain on any of the numerous monumentally heavy and confusing works trying to unravel the conspiracy behind the Kennedy assassination. Don't let the summary provided in *Mind Bombs* make you think you know it all already – it's a marvellous story.

A decent companion piece to the above would be Professor David Wrone's *The Zapruder Film: Reframing JFK's Assassination* (University of Kansas Press, 2003), which does what it says on the tin. This is a comprehensive demolition of the various conspiracy debunkers as well as a fantastic guide to the key evidence in the JFK shooting. (The JFK case is the best way in to respectable conspiracy theory, so if you don't want to go there, leave it well alone.)

Prior to writing *Smear!* with Ramsay, Stephen Dorrill co-authored another book about parapolitics, which should be devoured by anyone who wants to know exactly how much grime the official version of events can conceal. *Honeytrap: The Secret Worlds of Stephen Ward* by Anthony Summers and Stephen Dorrill (Weidenfield and Nicholson, 1987) is a re-investigation of the Profumo affair that goes into depths you didn't think could exist about affairs you never suspected. The perfect companion piece to *Smear!*

Tim Slessor's *Ministries of Deception: Cover-ups in Whitehall* (Aurum Press, 2002) contains an excellent chapter laying bare the astounding chicanery that emptied Diego Garcia, not to mention chapters unpicking the deceptions behind official denials of Gulf War Syndrome and various other governmental capers.

Former MI5 agent David Shayler's *Spies, Lies and Whistleblowers* (The Book Guild, 2005) isn't by former MI5 agent David Shayler at all. It's by his partner Annie Machon, because Shayler is legally prevented from writing about his intelligence career. It is just about the best book ever published on the workings of MI5. Plus it has sexy pages of blacked-out text where MI5's lawyers insisted on bits being withheld anyway, and a cover photograph of Machon and Shayler himself, taking the piss out of MI5 by dressing up as James Bond.

Dirty Politics: Deception, Distraction and Democracy by Kathleen Hall Jamieson (Oxford University Press, 1992) is an important book: a US-centred look at the way in which the public is bamboozled blind by unscrupulous media-savvy politicians.

On political secrecy, Peter Oborne's *The Rise of Political Lying* (Free Press, 2005) is an excellent and concise guide to the way in which UK politics has become overgrown with media handling and dishonesty. His critique is as harsh on the media as it is on politicians – the two, he says, have become engaged in a battle in which the dirtiest fighter is most likely to win. His survey of political dishonesty focuses mainly on the UK's post-1997 period and leaves the dishonesty of previous Conservative administrations strangely neglected. But how, I ask you, could anyone resist a book with chapter titles that include: 'The lies, falsehoods, deceits, evasions and artfulness of Tony Blair'?

Freedom of Information laws around the planet are covered in *Blacked Out: Government Secrecy in the Information Age* by Alasdair Roberts (Cambridge University Press, 2006), detailing how very much more civilised citizens are than governments when either side wants to know things about the other. If that whets your appetite, then there are various privacy/FOI websites that you could profitably look at: <www.no2id.net> and <www.privacyinternational.com> are just two.

For social engineering, the work of Ivan Illich represents a provocative starting point. *Limits to Medicine* is a good start. Much of it is out-dated now, but parts of it are just coming into historical focus. You might like to try *Deschooling Society*, which can be read online at <http://reactor-core.org/deschooling.html>

Illich's counterpart on education is top American teacher John Taylor Gatto, whose assault on the hidden policies of social engineering in the classroom will be of interest to any ex-pupil who ever wondered why you all had to swap classrooms when the bell rang, rather than waiting for the relevant teacher to come to you. *The Underground History of American Education* can now be read online at <www.johntaylorgatto.com>, but the printed and illustrated version is a beautiful thing, besides being far more portable. Fortunately you can order that via the website too.

Further insights into the stage-management of reality are to be found in Larry Tye's biography of Edward Bernays (self-proclaimed founder of the public relations industry), *The Father of Spin* (Owl Books, 2002), and Vance Packard's now ancient but still relevant *The Hidden Persuaders* (various publishers since 1957).

Readers wanting to peer further behind the curtain are advised to get acquainted with the superstar anarchist philosopher Noam Chomsky, whose various books and recorded lectures are a guaranteed source of stimulation.

The dark(er) side of social engineering is covered in the only work to read on the computerisation of the Nazi Holocaust: Edwin Black's *IBM and the Holocaust* (Crown, 2001).

On the flipside, if you wonder why it is that people go along with all sorts of crazy ideas that turn out to be false, erroneous or downright stupid, you might enjoy Charles Mackay's 1841 classic *Extraordinary Popular Delusions and the Madness of Crowds*. There's a chapter on witch-hunts that will make uncomfortable reading for anyone following the alleged 'War on Terror'.

Greg Palast's high-octane journalism is pretty much the only truly vital reportage going on in the media's 'blind spots' today. His 'debriefing' of Jospeh Stiglitz, the sacked World bank insider, can be found in Chapter 4 of the astonishing *The Best Democracy Money Can Buy* (Constable Robinson, 2002). For an even gamier dessert, try his *Armed Madhouse* (Allen Lane, 2006).

If you really like having your intellect stimulated and startling ideas splashed around willy-nilly, the author for you is Charles Fort, the man after whom *Fortean Times* was named. Fort's four books – *The Book of the Damned*, *New Lands*, *Lo!* and *Wild Talents* are among the most profoundly witty (and deliberately cranky) works in the English language. Have a try-before-you-buy at the website of Mr X (his legal name): <www.resologist.net>

Speaking of unexplained phenomena, the (im)possibility of an afterlife probably isn't really the sort of thing you can learn about from books. But a good start if you're interested in the hereafter would be *Stiff: The Curious Lives of Human Cadavers* by Mary Roach (Viking, 2003), a very moving and extremely funny account of what can happen to you after you're dead, whether you want it to or not. It's also quite, quite tasteless in parts. Ever fancied a career as a stunt driver?

There, you see, that didn't hurt, did it?

Author note

Very many thanks to copy editor Wendy Toole, without whose eye for detail any number of silly errors would have crept into the text.

Ex-Duckworther Dan Hind took a punt by commissioning me to write *Mind Bombs*. I hope the results bear some resemblance to whatever it was we agreed on.

Current Duckworther Caroline McArthur was a patient counsellor throughout months of revision (and didn't laugh in my face at the pitifulness of my first draft).

Deepest thanks to all three of you.

Lastly, if you want to drop me a line about anything you've read – or not read – or think you should have read – or shouldn't have read – in *Mind Bombs*, emails (subject line: 'mind bombs') should be directed to garrick23@hotmail.com.

In December 2006, students on the BA (Hons) Illustration course at the University of Brighton entered a competition to design the cover of *Mind Bombs*. We would like to thank the students who submitted their designs to us, and congratulate David Wilson, the winner of the competition. Thanks also to the course tutors at the University of Brighton, and to Russell at compoundEye Design for overseeing the project.

This

Index

is *humbly dedicated*

to

RICHARD ALEXANDER

and alſo to

The *ſtudious* and *Inquiring* Mind,

That any ſuch perſon will not be thought

An **IGNORAMUS** or yet

an **DULLARD**

at the Latter Daye,

To the righteous ſ**CORN** of thoſe

who *Betooke* themſelves

of the **trouble**

Of LEARNING

The thinges that it is

NEEDFUL

To Know,

newly *Reſearched* and *Compil'd*

Over Many

WEEKES

of

Effort and DILIGENCE

And at no little

TROUBLE or *EXPENſE*

to Your

ſincere

and

Humble

AUTHOR

Index

Index

Index

The Things They Say (reprise)

"As the state has claimed more power, the individual has seen his or her rights progressively eroded. The government that has made so much of setting the people free has claimed new powers at their expense [...] Britain is a more centralised state than ever before, more centralised than Germany, Italy, America or France. [...] So what has happened to civil rights over these ten years? First the Government has been prepared to allow the erosion of such basic rights as the well-established rights to free association and free expression. Secondly the state has increased its powers at the expense of the individual and strengthened the power of its officials without any real increase in their accountability. [...] There is no right to privacy, or anything approaching it, in Britain. An estimated 30,000 telephones are tapped.[...] Information on individuals is now compiled and held on an unprecedented scale, and no proper right of redress exists. That information may be inaccurate or improperly disclosed but there is little the offended individual can do. Many are concerned by the huge amount of unchecked information held on the Police National Computer and there is widespread and proper anxiety about black-listing. [...]"

— Gordon Brown MP lists some of his concerns in his attack on Thatcherism, *"Where There is Greed"* (1989)

The Which Blair Project (reprise)

"Several personality traits stand out very obviously. First, his early passion was not politics but performing. Actor-politicians tend to be especially narcissistic – which makes the hero role almost irresistible.

A second trait concerns his view of himself, in that he thinks he is always good. Someone who believes they cannot act badly will also believe that they cannot lie, so shading the truth can easily become a habit.

Linked to this is the nature of Blair's religious beliefs and the particular way he sees his relationship with God. In a television interview two years ago, he said, in relation to Iraq: "If you have faith about these things then you realise that judgment is made by other people. If you believe in God, it's made by God as well."

The implication is that the accountability that really matters to Blair is not to the electorate but to God. If, however, he is already convinced of his own goodness, that accountability is not constraining as it would be to the believer aware of his own capacity to sin. The belief in God becomes a spur to hubris rather than a constraint on it. No scientific explanation for hubris syndrome has yet been found and no such explanation may ever be found. However, watching the changes in the new sciences of the mind in my lifetime, as a former neurologist and politician, I believe they may ultimately provide an explanation of why some leaders succumb to hubris syndrome while others do not.

It may be that it never has a medical cure or even a proven medical causation, but it is becoming ever clearer that, as much as or even more than conventional illness, it is a great menace to the quality of leadership and the proper government of our world."

— Lord Owen (Dr David Owen): *"In Sickness and in Power: Illness in Heads of Government During the Last 100 Years"* (2008)

La, la, la, not listening (reprise)

"I and thousands like me have forsaken everything for what we believe [...] Your democratically elected governments continually perpetrate atrocities against my people all over the world. Your support makes you directly responsible. We are at war and I am a soldier. Now you too will taste the reality of this situation."

— Videoed 'martydom' statement of London bomber Mohammed Sidique Khan, July 2005

"Two-thirds of Britons believe there is a link between Tony Blair's decision to invade Iraq and the London bombings despite government claims to the contrary [...][V]oters believe further attacks in Britain by suicide bombers are also inevitable, with 75 per cent of those responding saying there will be more attacks. The research suggests the government is losing the battle to persuade people that terrorist attacks on the UK have not been made more likely by the invasion of Iraq. According to the poll, 33 per cent of Britons think the prime minister bears 'a lot' of responsibility for the London bombings and a further 31% "a little". Only 28 per cent of voters agree with the government that Iraq and the London bombings are not connected. The poll follows repeated efforts by the government to stress that al-Qaida attacks, including September 11, took place before, as well after, the invasion of Iraq. [...] The foreign secretary, Jack Straw, dismissed a thinktank report which argued that there was a link between the invasion of Iraq and the bombings. The report by Chatham House, formerly the Royal Institute of International Affairs, said: "There is no doubt that the situation over Iraq has imposed particular difficulties for the UK, and for the wider coalition against terrorism.""

— The Guardian, 19 July 2005

"Contributing to the agency's official website after the July 7 bombings, under the heading "Threat to the UK from international terrorism", a team of MI5 analysts concludes: "Though they have a range of aspirations and 'causes', Iraq is a dominant issue for a range of extremist groups and individuals in the UK and Europe." After the suicide bombings in London, Jack Straw, the Foreign Secretary, said there was no connection between them and the war in Iraq. This conflicted with a leaked assessment by the Joint Terrorism Analysis Centre, based at MI5 and run by a Ministry of Defence official, which claimed, three weeks before July 7 that Iraq was continuing to act "as a focus of a range of terroristrelated activities in Britain".

— *The Times*, 28 July 2005

"I do accept that people, of course, want to know exactly what happened and we will make sure that they do. We will bring together all the evidence that we have and we will publish it so that people, the victims and others, can see exactly what happened. But I really believe that at the present time, if we ended up having a full scale public inquiry when actually we do essentially know what happened on July 7, we would end up diverting a massive amount of police and security service time and I don't think it would be sensible."

— Tony Blair, in the House of Commons, 14 December 2005

"In the Commons yesterday, Tony Blair said an independent inquiry [into the London bombings] would "undermine support" for the security service."

— *The Guardian*, 3 May 2007

See also: Ecclesiastes 1:9

"A FALSE report, if it be believed during three days, may be of great service to a government." This political maxim has been ascribed to Catherine de Medici, an adept in *coups d'etat*, the *arcana imperii*! Between solid lying and disguised truth there is a difference known to writers skilled in the 'the art of governing mankind by deceiving them; as politics, ill-understood, have been described, and as, indeed, all party-politics are. These forgers perfer to use the truth disguised to the gross fiction. When the real truth can no longer be concealed, then they can confidently refer to it; for they can still explain and obscure, while they secure on their side the party whose cause they have advocated. A curious reader of history may discover the temporary and sometimes the lasting advantages of spreading rumours designed to disguise or to counteract the real state of things. Such reports, set a going, serve to break down the sharp and fatal point of a panic, which might instantly occur; In this way, the public is saved from the horrors of consternation, and the stupefaction of despair. These rumours give a breathing time to prepare for the disaster, which is doled out cautiously; and, as might be shown, in some cases these reports have left an event in so ambiguous a state, that a doubt may still arise whether these reports were really destitute of truth. Such reports, once printed, enter into history and perplex the honest historian."

"Of False Political Reports" — Isaac D'Israeli,
Curiosities of Literature (1839)